# Raising Children
## The Primary Years

**Everything parents need to know – from homework and horrid habits to screen time and sleepovers**

Liat Hughes Joshi

**with Dr Jemma Rosen-Webb
and Dr Harriet Tenenbaum**

**Prentice Hall Life**
is an imprint of

Harlow, England • London • New York • Boston • San Francisco • Toronto • Sydney • Singapore • Hong Kong
Tokyo • Seoul • Taipei • New Delhi • Cape Town • Madrid • Mexico City • Amsterdam • Munich • Paris • Milan

Pearson Education Limited

Edinburgh Gate
Harlow CM20 2JE
Tel: +44 (0)1279 623623
Fax: +44 (0)1279 431059
Website: www.pearsoned.co.uk

First published in Great Britain in 2011

© Pearson Education 2011

The right of Liat Hughes Joshi to be identified as author of this work has been asserted by her in accordance with the Copyright, Designs and Patents Act 1988.

Pearson Education is not responsible for the content of third party internet sites.

ISBN: 978-0-273-73051-4

*British Library Cataloguing-in-Publication Data*
A catalogue record for this book is available from the British Library

*Library of Congress Cataloging-in-Publication Data*
Joshi, Liat Hughes.
    Raising children, the primary years : everything parents need to know--from homework and horrid habits to screen time and sleepovers / Liat Hughes Joshi, with Jemma Rosen-Webb and Harriet Tenenbaum.
        p. cm.
    Includes bibliographical references and index.
    ISBN 978-0-273-73051-4 (pbk. : alk. paper) 1. Child rearing. 2. Parenting.
    I. Rosen-Webb, Jemma. II. Tenenbaum, Harriet. III. Title.
    HQ769.J7/5 2011
    649'.1--dc22

                            2010037976

The publisher is grateful to Kidscape (www.kidscape.org.uk) for permission to reproduce the safety guidelines on page 121, taken from www.kidscape.org.uk/assets/downloads/kskeepthemsafe.pdf

10 9 8 7 6 5 4 3 2 1
14 13 12 11 10

Typeset in 11/15.5pt Classical Garamond BT by 3
Printed in Great Britain by Henry Ling Ltd, at the Dorset Press, Dorchester, Dorset

# Contents

# About the author

Liat Hughes Joshi is a parenting journalist who contributes to national newspapers and magazines. Prior to her second career as a writer, Liat spent 9 long, exhausting years as a management consultant in the City (during which time she actually did about 15 years' worth of work). She is also the author of *What to Buy for Your Baby* and lives in north London with her husband and son.

## About the child psychologists

Our two main child psychologists have contributed to various chapters, depending on their research interests and experience.

Dr Jemma Rosen-Webb trained as a clinical psychologist at the University of East London. She worked in the NHS for nine years before moving to the USA, where she currently lives and works.

She specialises in helping children and families, ranging from one-off consultations on everyday issues, to regular meetings over a longer period, where there are more significant concerns. The issues discussed in this book often come up with the families she assists with.

Dr Harriet Tenenbaum received a PhD in child developmental psychology from the University of California,

Santa Cruz and completed a postdoctoral fellowship at the Harvard Graduate School of Education. She is a reader at Kingston University where she teaches and conducts research on aspects of child psychology. Harriet is a mother of one and lives in southwest London.

# Acknowledgements

Special thanks to super psychologists Jemma and Harriet, and publishers Elie and Rachael.

Thanks too to my long-suffering husband for enduring my rantings and being a fantastic unpaid editor. To Roni Jay, Niyati Keni, Lillian Wilkinson, Sarah Wild and Julia Nicholson for your ideas and input through the two years I worked on this book.

To my own lovely primary schooler, Luca, for inadvertently being my inspiration.

And finally, to my grandmother for her unconditional support since the days when it was me going to primary school, and before.

# Introduction

Visit the parenting section of any large bookshop and you'll find shelves groaning under the weight of guides to babies, toddlers and teens, yet a curious lack of anything about the years in between.

So is this post-toddler, pre-teen period blissfully easy? As soon as they set foot through a school gate for the first time, do they morph into perfect children, only reverting back to being more challenging once they're well into double digits?

Parents of primary-school children – and I'm guessing that if you're reading this, that's you as well as me – know darn well this simply and sadly isn't the case. Yes 4–11-year-olds can be fabulous, fun and funny, and no, they're not quite as exhausting as screaming-for-a-feed-all-night babies or stroppy-rebellious-I-hate-you-Mum/Dad teens, but they're no walk in the parenting park either.

This book addresses all those little, and not so little, challenges you might face with your primary schooler, taking each issue and providing background information, experts' views, and practical, realistic advice on what to do about it.

There are armfuls of tips from our wonderful panel of parents, drawn from all over the UK and beyond. They've been there, done that and have the worry lines to show for it, so you can learn the easy (or at least easier) way to deal with all this stuff.

Sometimes there's more than one approach to an issue – intentionally, as all families are different, all children are different and every scenario will vary slightly. Pick/ choose what you think might work best for your individual situation. You might need to persist with changes for more than a couple of days.

Chapters are split by themes – from food, sleep and school stuff to sex, drugs and rock and roll (OK, maybe not the last one). There's advice on everything from getting them to eat their bloody veg to, ahem, stopping them from swearing. There's also a catch-all 'other stuff' chapter for issues too important to be left out but which didn't fit neatly elsewhere.

Whilst you can read the book from cover to cover if you like, it's designed so you, no doubt a busy parent, can dip in and out, using it as a reference guide when you come up against a specific problem.

I hope that from this book you'll not only get practical ways to improve life with your primary schooler but also be reassured that what they're up to (probably) is normal and that you (probably) aren't rubbish parents who are getting it all wrong. Even if it feels that way when you've had seven arguments and aren't even halfway through half term yet.

## The expert panel

As well as our two main child psychologists, Dr Jemma Rosen-Webb and Dr Harriet Tenenbaum, a few other experts were dragged in to advise on specific issues, notably Michelle Elliot of anti-bullying and child-safety charity

Kidscape, nutritionist Sally Child, child psychologist and author Dr Pat Spungin, and Professor Susan Hallam of the Institute of Education.

## The parent panel

Parents of primary-school children from all over the country have contributed their experiences, advice and ideas, completing over 400 surveys. Initially, they were asked about their key issues for each chapter to ensure the book covers the right stuff. They provided answers to questions you might not feel comfortable swapping notes on in the playground without seeming nosey; and, most importantly, they've shared their own tips and advice.

Next to their quotes, their children's ages are listed as at the time of the survey for the chapter concerned and we've usually excluded mentioning any siblings who are under 4 or over 11.

Special thanks to the following parent panellers:

Sue and Katiya Tanner, Louise Betley, Kelly Wright, Hina Gadhia, Jo Barlow, Angila Kent, St Andrew's School PTA parents, Angela Green, Katrina 'G-S', Claire King, Amanda (and Bernadette and Thomas) Broomhall, Helen Cripps and Petra Davis. Many parents preferred to remain anonymous or didn't want their full names identifying due to the sometimes sensitive nature of their quotes – you know who you are – thank you too.

# 1

# General behaviour management for primary schoolers

This book has been written very much with specific issues in mind. However, underlying many of these are a general set of parenting principles which are worth keeping in mind.

They're not necessarily rocket science and probably not things you've never heard mention of before. They're simple principles, founded both in solid psychological theory and practical experience of what is effective for children this age.

Inevitably, there's no single way that works for every family, every child and every situation, but, on the whole, a basic approach to behaviour management for this age group is:

## Tactic one: Reward and praise

Countless psychological studies have shown positive rewards are more effective for changing children's (and indeed adults') behaviour than punishment and other negative consequences.

Reward or star charts provide a framework for encouraging good behaviour generally and can also be used for specific problems, such as stopping nail biting or the trying of new foods.

There are two main ways they can work:

1   Have set categories and a star for each one at the end of the day. *If* they get enough stars they get a reward that day or credit towards a reward at the end of the week. Don't make it overly easy or overly difficult to get the reward, or the chart won't motivate them.

**2** Award stars or stickers on an ad hoc basis for good behaviour and then once they get a certain number on their chart, they get the reward. Some parents using this style of chart choose to remove stickers for 'bad' behaviour.

Personally, I prefer the set categories as it is clearer to the child what they need to do to get their rewards.

My son's chart's categories have included 'Tidying up toys at the end of the day' and 'Being quiet after lights out [at bedtime]'.

You can buy reward charts or download them for free on some websites, but equally you can just make one, potentially involving your child.

## Reward chart principles

- Make the categories specific, clear and measurable, e.g. 'Playing with your little brother for 20 minutes a day' rather than 'Playing with your little brother'.

- Involve them in a discussion about what their categories should be (although of course you get the final say).

- Keep targets realistic and achievable, e.g. for a vegetable-hater not to eat all their veg but just to try them.

- Change the categories over time as needed. As a new behaviour becomes ingrained, make it just what's expected and switch the category to something else.

- Do it daily – if you don't, it undermines the process.

- Younger children will need more regular rewarding (but the rewards can be smaller – at 5, my son was delighted to get a solitary Smartie!) Older ones can earn ticks, stickers or tokens daily to count towards a bigger treat at the end of the week.

- Work out what type of reward will press your child's buttons and, again, involve them (within reason). Will they be motivated by working towards extra pocket money to buy a particular toy/game? Or by additional attention from you, e.g. an extra bedtime story, or selecting the DVD you watch as a family at the weekend?

- Keep siblings' charts separate.

- Star charts are not great for dealing with behaviour that is difficult to monitor consistently such as swearing, lying or stealing. These are better managed through ignoring, discussions or reparations (see below).

## General praise principles

As discussed above, reward charts can be a powerful motivator, but good old-fashioned praise is immensely effective too.

Here are some principles for using praise well:

- Keep it specific – 'That's great' will have less effect than 'It was great that you tidied your bedroom/tried that broccoli'.

- You can't overdo praise where it's warranted (i.e. not just for breathing!) but try to put the emphasis on your child's effort rather than their end achievement or innate qualities such as 'being clever'. This will help them develop persistence with tasks they find difficult, rather than giving up and thinking 'That's just something I'm not good at'.

- Make sure it's genuine. Even fairly young children can spot overly fake praise.

- Praise at the time, although it won't hurt to mention something again later on as well to reinforce your message, e.g. in front of their teacher, grandparents or your partner.

## Tactic two: Ignore

Some behaviour from primary schoolers is very much intended to wind you up or get your attention (even if it's not necessarily *good* attention). If this is the case *and* the behaviour is fairly minor (e.g. mild swearing), your most powerful weapon is not to react at all. This might require deep breaths/covert fist clenching/leaving the room on your part, and is tough but it can pay off.

If it's a behaviour you can't totally ignore, then in a short, matter-of-fact manner, say it's something you don't like them doing and you'll be ignoring them until they stop, or similar.

Ignoring means taking away both verbal and non-verbal attention. Focus on something/someone else and avoid further discussions about why you don't want them to do whatever it is.

It is, however, really important to give your attention back as soon as they stop the behaviour. This might only be a split second, e.g. a break in whining, but if you manage to do this, it will reinforce the way you want them to behave.

## Tactic three: Remove

Sometimes ignoring the bad and rewarding the good isn't appropriate if your child does something graver like hitting/being aggressive.

Time out works well for some parents for this sort of thing but personally I'm not a huge fan as it so easily turns into a very stressful battle, with you dragging your child to the step/their room. If you *do* do it, the idea is one minute for each year of their age and the time-out zone should be pretty boring.

Instead of time out, the removal of an important item or privilege for a set, appropriate period can be very effective. It could be that you say 'If you don't stop doing X and start doing Y, there will be no TV today', or you will put away that cherished game/toy for the rest of the day.

### *Principles for removal of a privilege or item*

- It needs to be something they *really* like, the removal of which will be proportionate to the misdemeanour. It shouldn't, however, be an item of comfort such as a bedtime teddy bear.

- You *must* always follow through with your threat, and take the action quickly after whatever they've done.

- You must not let them have it back early, no matter how much they whine/beg/plead.

This tactic does rely on there being a single possession/ privilege that will be missed. So 'If you don't stop doing X, I'll take Y away for the rest of the day' really won't work if they aren't so fussed about Y and will just play with other toys. Again, you have to find out what presses their buttons – there will almost certainly be something.

## Other primary parenting principles and tips

The following are also worth considering with this age group:

- Children (and adults) don't process words like 'don't' and 'not' as well as positive ones. Therefore when your child is doing something you'd rather they didn't, try to think what it is you *do* want them to do and tell them this. So, instead of 'Don't run' say 'Walk next to me'; instead of 'You're shovelling your food in' say 'Make sure you chew your food well'. Be clear and specific.

- Calm, non-shouty explanations of the consequences of their behaviour can be surprisingly effective. For example, 'If you don't stop messing around and get off to sleep you'll be too tired to enjoy football tomorrow'.

- Ensure your expectations are fair and appropriate for them as individuals and for their age/development.

- Try to keep things fun – make a game of chores or get them to race to see who can get dressed quickest in the morning. Often there are imaginative, fun solutions to problems which can keep the mood lighter.

- A dose of humour can defuse tense moments. That's not to say you should start joking in the middle of telling your offspring off – there's a time and a place, obviously.

- Play the 'You're so grown-up' card – especially with the younger end of the age range. Little kids love to be told they're so grown-up, for the same reason many of them add halves and quarters on when giving their age.

- You can be their friend but ultimately you're in charge. Modern parenting consults and involves children more than in the past but you can take this too far. Kids need boundaries and firmness. Our job as parents is to guide them and nurture them into becoming balanced, functioning adults. With some decisions the buck stops with you, even if they don't like it and perhaps won't like you for it.

- There are two types of fairness – real fairness and a child's perceived view of fairness. So when they whinge 'That's sooo not fair', often it's just their way of complaining. If you find yourself saying 'Because I'm your parent/a grown-up/because I say so' too often without a strong explanation about why, have a think about what's going on and whether what you're expecting is fair. It's easy to behave inconsistently, e.g. if you swear but then say to your child they can't.

- Never plead. It just doesn't work with most children. If I plead with my son to do something, it's one of the quickest ways to ensure he won't.

- Lead by example. Children copy their parents. If you shout a lot, they will probably shout a lot too. We're all human, we all shout sometimes, but if you don't want your child to be generally shouty/aggressive/over-sensitive, do look at how you react to things, as you are their biggest guide.

- Think about the balance of positive and negative comments you make to and about them. No one likes to be criticised all day. If you're always telling your child off, take a step back. Try to break the pattern and you might end up surprised – telling them they're behaving nicely (when they are) could become self-fulfilling.

- Watch out for the threat of the hollow threat. Never declare that you'll do X unless you really will do X. There's the classic 'Father Christmas won't bring you any presents unless you're good'. This sort of thing is often said in the heat of the moment, but the problem is even one hollow threat undermines your authority when you make statements like this in future.

- Drop some of the little things. Griping about minor issues can really make children feel you're always on at them, making tackling bigger problems harder. And frankly it's probably stressful for you. Ask yourself, does it really matter if they, say, put their elbows on the table or act a bit silly sometimes?

- Recognise that peer pressure can be huge for school-age children. Sometimes it's good to teach them not to go with the crowd but occasionally it's worth letting them have/do something you're not that keen on but don't absolutely oppose, if it helps them fit in.

- Never cave in to whining! It might be easier at the time but you'll open the door to the idea that whining works and will probably hear a lot more of it as a consequence.

- Recognise that sometimes with changes there's short-term pain before long-term gain. Solving a problem might well mean effort for a while but chances are things will get better. In the long run it'll be worth it. If it's something to do with eating or sleeping, and you know it's going to be taxing for a few days whilst you fix things, choose a period when you've got more support or are all going to be relatively relaxed. It might be during school holidays or when your partner's home from work for a few days.

- Try to show a united front with your partner – hard though it can be, put discussions about issues such as how to discipline your kids on hold until later so you won't undermine each other.

- Consider setting 'family rules' – sit down together and agree them. Put them up on the fridge. Stick with them yourselves too.

- None of us is perfect, all families get shouty and annoyed with each other at least occasionally. Sometimes it's wise to walk away from your children for a few minutes. If they're safe and things are getting out of hand, leave them to it until you and they calm down.

And finally:

- If all else fails, remember it's (probably) only a phase, but it will pass. But remember this applies to the good things as well as the bad – so enjoy these years.

# 2
# Friends and foes

## Friendship problems, sleepovers, bullying and playdates

## The big issues

- ✔ Trouble making friends
- ✔ Falling out
- ✔ Bullying
- ✔ Undesirable friends
- ✔ Playdates – your house, your rules?
- ✔ Sleepovers

Regardless of whether your child is the life and soul of the birthday-party circuit or struggles socially, primary-school friendships can be a minefield. You've got to work out how to discipline visiting children in your house, decide what to do about any 'less desirable' friends, somehow ensure they fall asleep before 2am during sleepovers, proffer shoulders to cry on when they fall out and advise those struggling to make friends in the first place.

Look on the bright side: after all this playground diplomacy, if you ever apply for a job as a UN peacekeeper, you'll be highly qualified.

# Trouble making friends

If yours is the child who sits alone on the playground edge or is always left off party-invite lists, it can be heart-wrenching for both of you. Struggling to make friends can harm a child's happiness, self-esteem and even academic performance. Clearly sometimes difficulties building friendships sit alongside bullying, but not always, so we address the two issues separately.

## Background info

Academic research suggests around 10 per cent of children have no friends in their class and are disliked by their peers.

## What the child psychologist says

Dr Jemma Rosen-Webb:

> 'It can be incredibly painful to see your child being rejected or not included in play by others. There are several reasons why a child might struggle to form friendships. Some children may know "how" to socialise and be able to play well with siblings and children they know but when it comes to talking to other children they do not know well, or in larger group settings, they may feel shy and find it harder to find ways to join in. Or it could be they are aggressive (sometimes due to underdeveloped language, play or social skills – e.g. turn taking, making conversation) or have difficulties regulating emotions. For some children it might just be that they haven't had as much opportunity to practise being social.'

## What you can do about it

**Use 'playdates' to promote new friendships or strengthen existing ones** Sometimes it can be tempting not to bother inviting kids over if the issues your child is having make things tricky, but persevering is normally worthwhile. If playdates don't work the way you've been doing them so far, try providing more structured activities, or changing the duration or venue (e.g. meeting out rather than at their/your house).

*'When my daughter was having problems making friends, I encouraged playdates and suggested she take in a game to play at school. I also reminded her that children will want to play with her if they see she's happy and having fun.'*

Susan (daughter 9, sons 11 and 7)

**Observe their interactions with other children** Watch how they behave with other kids – are they very shy, aggressive or bossy? If so, discuss this with them afterwards and work out what they could do differently. Role play can be beneficial for this. If they're aggressive, work on ways to express their emotions differently. Give clear and specific praise when they behave in a more appropriate way.

*'I talked about the problems he has. He's not shy but he can wind other kids up without realising, e.g. trying to take over their games. So I've talked through these things with him and tried to get him to see how he can help himself.'*

Marcia (sons 11, 9 and 6)

**Talk to their teacher** A teacher should have an idea of what is going on during school hours and of any issues which are causing your child to struggle with friendships. There might be someone in class who they feel is similar to your child and he/she might be able to encourage things along. Ask if there's a scheme in the school playground for children looking for a playmate, e.g. a 'friendship bench' and if there isn't, suggest one.

*'I spoke with her teacher and asked if she could encourage more interaction with the girls in the class, which did make quite a difference.'*

Sarah (daughters 9, 8 and 5)

**Encourage non-school friendships via activities and family friends** If your youngster is shy or has different interests from others at school, out-of-school activities could be a better source of friendships, and making friends in another setting should boost their confidence. This might in turn help them with school friendships too.

**Recognise that some children are actually content with their own company or just one or two friends**

*'Although he does have some friends, I know he's pretty happy playing by himself more than most children are and have learnt to accept that he isn't the life and soul. If he's OK with that, I am too.'*

Anna (son 7, daughter 6)

**Seek further advice** If your child has ongoing difficulties with social communication, understanding social rules and/or making friends, seek further advice. Talk to the school again and/or your GP as a starting point.

# Falling out

*'Every day it appears T and the other children in the class have fallen out with someone and then they are best friends again the day after.'*

Especially in the early years of primary school, children seem to fall in and out with each other almost as quickly as a round of Hokey Cokey. Even if you know it'll probably be forgotten tomorrow, it's not easy consoling a heart-broken child.

Later on, older kids' friendships do usually stabilise but then when 'break-ups' happen they tend to be more serious and it's harder to replace lost pals because others in the class have more established relationships.

## Background info

Falling out with friends is a very common occurrence. Of our parent panel's children, 68 per cent had had a serious bust-up with a buddy at some stage. Girls seem to have more fallings-out than boys.

## What the child psychologist says

Dr Jemma Rosen-Webb:

> 'Children's friendships and their understanding of others develop through a few stages. Younger ones understand the world in terms of fixed states such as "right and wrong", "good and bad". They are unlikely to think from other people's perspectives and there is no middle ground – either someone is their friend or not. Someone doing something they don't like can easily throw them into the "not my friend" category, only to be reinstated as "friend" again soon after.
>
> If children's understanding of social relationships is nurtured and develops appropriately, for example by caregivers helping them think about other people's perspectives, then by the

age of 7 or 8 they start to show an increased ability to do this for themselves. As they gain a better understanding of other people's feelings and perspectives, they begin to act in ways that may be more about fulfilling other's needs than their own: "I'd do it because it would make her happy". They also become better able to understand and cope with the middle ground. For example, an older child might feel hurt by something a friend said or did and show annoyance but understand (probably still with some help) that people we like sometimes make mistakes and hurt us. As a result, they are better equipped to come up with alternatives to dismissing the friendship altogether. Children need to learn skills to solve their own problems – so find ways to facilitate this. It can be tempting to jump in and solve disagreements for them but they will learn more from being helped to find their own solutions.'

## What you can do about it

**Listen and provide guidance** Even if you know it will probably all be resolved tomorrow, it's important to them right now and it's comforting to know you are there to listen. Acknowledge how they might feel and ask what they think they might be able to do about it. Give ideas on this as well.

> 'We discussed her telling the particular friend that she doesn't want to be bossed around and telling her that they both need to decide things together. We even did a little role play of this.'
>
> Anna (son 7, daughter 6)

**But let them work it out themselves with their friend wherever possible** (They'll learn a useful skill for life.) It's not wise to phone the parents or try and solve it directly initially, although this might be needed later on. If so, keep things factual with the other parent so they don't feel you're criticising their beloved child too much!

> *'We try not to intervene – normally after 24 hours they are all friends again. If it went on longer, then we would. It's a lesson in life – learning how to manage friendships – and to interfere too much would ruin that lesson.'*
>
> Heather (daughter 8)

> *'I talk to them to make sure that they are okay and it is not a serious problem but otherwise leave them to make up and then fall out again – they always seem to work it out.'*
>
> Sharon (sons 10 and 8)

# Bullying

*'The bullying went on for most of 2 years, up to year 2. S became depressed and did badly at school. His behaviour declined and he was labelled as the naughty kid. It was a nightmare.'*

Bullying is an unpleasant fact of all too many children's lives and an upsetting issue for parents to contend with. Fortunately most (maybe not all) schools and teachers take bullying much more seriously than in the past, with policies, earlier intervention and more advice available on how to help.

## Background info

Bullying is very common, although statistics vary depending on how you define it. Government figures suggest a quarter of primary-school children are victims at some stage.

## What the expert on bullying says

Michele Elliot of the anti-bullying charity Kidscape (www.kidscape.org.uk):

'Bullying isn't always easy to define. It can be emotional, physical or verbal. Children who bully may seem to focus on one presumed characteristic of a child. However, do remember that a child's alleged "difference" is not really the point of the bullying – bullies are playing with power. Children who are bright are often bullied, as are children with learning differences; tall children are bullied, so are small ones.

Persistent bullying can result in shyness, low self-esteem, depression, poor academic performance and even threatened or actual suicide.

There are all sorts of signs to look out for that your child might be being bullied. They might be unwilling to go to school, feel ill in the mornings, begin doing poorly in schoolwork, come home regularly with books or clothes damaged or missing, or become distressed or anxious. Other warning signs are if they become less confident, have unexplained cuts or bruises or they begin to bully others.'

## What you can do about it

**Be someone to turn to and a shoulder to cry on** Don't dismiss what they feel or conversely make them talk about it more than they want to.

> '*I let them know that it wasn't OK and I would do everything I could to stop it. I encouraged them to talk to me about it, got advice from experts and read books about how to help.*'
>
> Marcia (sons 11, 9 and 6)

> '*Don't pressure your child into talking about it but give lots of opportunities for discussion (at the dinner table/ bedtime).*'
>
> Carol (daughters 8 and 6)

**Provide your child with ways to deal with minor issues themselves** (Although they might not always seem minor to your child.)

Discuss ways of staying calm if it happens again (e.g. deep breaths, thinking about people who they love, imagining a force field that does not let words hurt them). If it's some mild name-calling, perhaps suggest a few clever retorts or ignoring and pretending the comments don't bother them. My favourite – from a post on an internet parenting site – was this, suggested by a mum whose child had been called a geek: 'Yes, but Bill Gates is a geek and he's the richest man in the world'. I bet that shut the little blighters up.

**Discuss persistent or more significant bullying with the school** Keeping a diary of incidents on your child's behalf might help a teacher understand the scale and nature of the problem.

*'Absolutely discuss it with school. In both cases [where my sons were being bullied] the schools took it very seriously, acted swiftly, and managed to stop it.'*

Marcia (sons 11, 9 and 6)

**Think very carefully about approaching the bully's parents directly** It's almost always better to go to the school rather than the other parents unless you know them really well (even then, this is an emotive issue, so proceed with caution!).

*'I didn't talk to the parents of the bully – his mum would have been mortified and she is a very nice woman.'*

Marina (son 8, daughter 4)

*'The other parents didn't want to listen.'*

Rachel (son 8)

**Help build their self-esteem** If your child is bullied at school, encourage non-school friendships, perhaps via out-of-school activities. And keep telling them how much you love them/think they're special and why.

Other ways to bolster self-esteem include reminding them that it's not their fault, that it's more likely about the bully's insecurities and that they are not alone – you are there for them.

**Remind them that bullies are less likely to bully if they don't get a reaction** I wish someone had told me this when

I was at school – many bullies pile in if they see it's getting to you.

---

**If your child is the bully**

If your child is bullying others, you are not alone: one survey suggested around a third of boys (35 per cent) and a quarter of girls (26 per cent) admit they have bullied other children 'a little' or 'a lot'.

Being the parents of a bully can be awkward, embarrassing and worrying. Get the facts about what's happened – it's important not to turn a blind eye – even if it's hard to believe your little angel is the perpetrator. Talk with them about why bullying is wrong and its impact, about how they'd feel if they were on the receiving end, and work with school to solve the problem.

Again role playing could be useful here. Most of all try and understand why they are bullying as there might well be an underlying reason that you need to resolve.

---

# Undesirable friends

There's at least one in every class – the kid you dread your son or daughter befriending. So what if it happens, what if they come home and say 'Can I go to [insert name of monster child]'s house to play?' Your heart sinks, you don't want the other child leading yours 'astray'!

Do you ban them from visiting and discourage the friendship? Do you explain to your child why you don't want them to be friends (but risk them being drawn all the more to Little Master or Miss Unsuitable and contribute to labelling the child concerned or it being repeated to them that 'My mum said …')? Or should you keep your disapproval quiet, let them become best mates and hope for the best, that your child doesn't get drawn into a life of crime/drugs/saying the F word every sentence?

## Background info

The main reasons why the parent panel viewed a particular child as an unsuitable friend were:

- swearing
- aggression
- being allowed age-inappropriate activities at home, e.g. violent films or inappropriate video games.

## What the child psychologist says

Dr Jemma Rosen-Webb:

'Remember some children act up because they are not getting enough positive attention at home and/or have not had enough opportunities to learn how to enjoy time with other children. Others have difficulties with attention and social skills.

If your child wants to be friends with someone you are unsure about, consider giving them a chance but perhaps keep playtimes short and structured to begin with. You may want to make sure you are close by to guide them through any conflicts or inappropriate language or behaviour, e.g. playing a board game all together. Fundamentally, though, do not let your child visit a home that you do not feel comfortable with them being in.'

## What you can do about it

**Either don't intervene at all and grin and bear it ...** (Unless there's something truly dangerous involved, of course.)

> *'I didn't do anything. My daughter is allowed to have her own friends, even ones I would rather she didn't.'*
>
> Susan (daughter 9, sons 11 and 7)

> *'Just leave them to it and keep your fingers crossed!'*
>
> Claire (daughter 5)

**... or subtly obstruct things and guide them towards more appropriate friends**

> *'I'm making excuses not to invite [the undesirable friend] to playdates. The connection is wearing off and hopefully this child will drift on to someone else. I go for gentle manipulation towards kids you want them to play with.'*
>
> Frankie (son 4)

> *'I generally find that if I'm not cooperating with invitations to play, etc., things usually ease off. I did tell my son that if one particular friend came over again, I would hold him responsible for keeping the house tidy and the toys unbroken. He hasn't asked to have the child over to play since.'*
>
> Marcia (sons 11, 9 and 6)

**Be wary of showing too much disapproval** This can make the attraction of the 'undesirable one' all the more magnetic!

Sometimes it's not the child that's the problem but what goes on at their house when your child visits. If it's something minor and easy to solve, e.g. you'd rather he/she didn't eat so much chocolate, of course it's fine to politely mention it to the other parents.

For more serious issues, you've little choice but to face the awkward task of not letting them go there again and potentially having to explain why to the other parents and your child. Watch what you actually say to your son or daughter as, of course, it might well get repeated; and be careful about making excuses if your son or daughter knows they aren't true. Perhaps keep it to a simple 'X's parents have different rules and I'm not comfortable with that' and answer any questions in a reasonably matter-of-fact way, e.g. 'X is allowed to do that but we'd prefer you not to'.

# Playdates – your house, your rules?

There might be a fairly new-fangled term for what used to merely be called 'having someone round to play' but there's an enduring issue: how do you discipline other people's misbehaving kids in your house? Should you expect the same rules to apply to visiting children as you do to your own or relax them a bit? Should you spill the beans at picking-up time and tell the other parents about their darling angel's devilish behaviour?

## Background info

- Disciplining 'visiting kids' is almost universally disliked by the parent panel and makes many feel uncomfortable.

- A 'my house, my rules' approach is taken by 66 per cent, with all the same rules applying as to their own children, while 34 per cent enforce major rules such as no hitting but relax others, e.g. table manners.

## What the child psychologist says

Dr Jemma Rosen-Webb:

'Families vary greatly in the way they bring up children. Be realistic about what is fair to expect of a child who is a guest in your home. Different rules may seem unusual, unfair, confusing or unsettling to them. Think about which rules are absolutes (usually no hurting others and not destroying property) and which you could relax a little, e.g. table manners.

Try to frame rules that you do need to be clear on, such as "In this house/family we don't ..." and give them alternatives that they can do instead, e.g. "In this house we don't draw on the walls but there is some paper over here if you'd like to draw on that". Even better, frame rules in terms of what is expected rather than what is not expected: "We all stay at the table until everyone has finished eating". Make sure you physically get down to their level so you can make eye contact, and try to stay calm – towering above children can be intimidating and their anxiety may result in further disruptive behaviour.

Do not worry too much if you relax some of your less significant rules for the other child or yours while they have friends over, e.g. letting them eat in front of the TV when they are not normally allowed to. As long as you are consistent with your rules at other times, your child will learn to discriminate between different situations.'

## What you can do about it

**Stand firm about enforcing your normal 'major' rules with visiting kids** It is your house and as long as it's something reasonable and you make them aware of it, it's fair to ask them to stick with your rules.

> 'For the big stuff like no hitting, if you're in my house you follow the rules like everyone else. I expect my kids to do as they're told when they're with someone else and the same applies here.'
>
> Vic (daughter 5)

> 'They will be "gently" reminded about the way we expect them to behave. At the end of the day we can exercise the right not to invite them back.'
>
> Heather (daughter 8)

> 'Why should they get away with things that my children can't? It gives a mixed message to them and so I try and stick to the house rules as much as I can. If a child is in my care, I have a duty to ensure they are safe and if that means "having a word" if they are pushing the boundaries, then so be it.'
>
> Sarah (daughters 9, 8 and 5)

**But deal with things a bit more gently** Remember, they just aren't used to your family's 'ways'.

> '[I enforce the same rules] to a degree, but with possibly more explaining in a calm manner, as they are not aware of my standards, unlike my children who have it drummed in (but still sometimes take no notice!).'
>
> Sarah (daughters 9, 8 and 5)

**Consider reminding children of house rules at the start of their visit** This is especially worthwhile if you suspect or know a child is prone to misbehaving.

**And if things get really bad ...** Don't be afraid to call the other parents to take their child home early (but see below about breaking the news) and/or threaten that they won't be allowed to visit again.

> *'If the child is really bad, I will tell them that they are being naughty, and that they either pack it in or I will take them home.'*
>
> Sophie (son 9)

> *'I tell them, and my child, they won't be allowed round again ... so go and think about it!'*
>
> Jo (son 10, daughter 8)

---

### Should you tell the other parents if their child misbehaved?

Say Chloe trashes your coffee table by drawing all over it, James tips a bottle of shampoo over the bathroom floor, or Alex persists in severe swearing even though you've told him to stop. Should you tell their parents at picking-up time?

The done thing and indeed the wise thing seems to be to tell the other parents only about more serious misdemeanours, choosing words and tone carefully. Reporting minor issues can sound gripey.

As Dr Jemma Rosen-Webb advises, there's a good chance the other parent will be embarrassed and possibly feel criticised by you. Here are her ideas on how to raise such issues:

- Use a 'positive-negative-positive sandwich' – tell them about something that went well or was enjoyable, follow it by the tricky event and finish with another positive. If the

---

other parent is feeling less criticised, they're more likely to listen to the bits that are harder to hear.

- Try to find ways to positively frame what happened, e.g. 'They were really involved in their play. Unfortunately she got a bit overexcited and ended up biting him.'
- Let the other parent know if it was difficult for you to know how to handle it and what you did. Then maybe ask them how they would like you to deal with it if there is a next time.

**What the parent panel do**

*'I usually do [tell the parents] but in a friendly way. I'll say "Oh, I ought to tell you I had to have a word with X because he was hurting the cat [or whatever]. It isn't a problem and he was as good as gold afterwards. I'm only mentioning it so that you know for when they tell you."'*
Susan (daughter 9, sons 11 and 7)

*'If it was terrible – fighting, say – and the other child got upset about it, I will mention it to their parents, so that they don't get the wrong story from their child. Children usually tell the story so that their parent is horrified, so it's best to get in there first!'*
Angila (daughter 6)

*'I think if children have done something mean and you know they did it, their parents should know and would want to. I never raise anything not seen by me in person though.'*
Kate (son 8, daughter 4)

# Sleepovers

*'Sleepovers invariably dissolve into a horrible muddle of exhausted and emotional small children – and adults for that matter.'*

Sleepovers can be fantastic fun for your children but having someone else's child stay overnight is quite a responsibility, certainly compared with having them pop round to play for an hour or two. There can be bedwetting, homesick kids wailing about missing mum at 2am and misplaced teddy bears. Then there's the biggest challenge of all: getting them to stop giggling/chatting/pillow fighting and start sleeping whilst the hour is still earthly. Maybe we should be renaming them 'awakeovers'? Far more appropriate given the amount of actual sleeping that typically goes on.

## Background info

According to our own survey, the age at which sleepovers were first held varied enormously – some children were pre-schoolers, others still hadn't started on them by age 11. Of those whose children had had one, 66 per cent held their first when they were 7 or under, whilst 34 per cent were 8 or over.

> 'We started with them at ours at about 4, she was reluctant to stay at others' houses but did do from about 6.'
>
> Toni (daughter 8, son 4)

> 'From year 5 – almost age 10, which is the rule in our family.'
>
> Jo (son 10, daughter 8)

> 'My daughter has her friends over one or two nights a month and has done since the age of about 7 or 8. My son has started in the last year.'
>
> Amanda (daughter 10, son 8)

**Sleepover rules**

Unsurprisingly, the parent panel confine sleepovers to weekends and holidays (a few say holidays only).

*'[They're only allowed] when there's no school the next day. I would be happy to have a child as a favour to a friend in urgent need of a babysitter during the week but I'd be strict about normal bed and sleep times.'*

Marcia (sons 11, 9 and 6)

Other rules vary but include:

*'Teeth! No name calling, no ridiculing of cuddlies or pyjama choice.'*

Kate (sons 8 and 4)

*'No TV or electronic games at bedtime/in bed. No going downstairs until 7am, and only after they have asked.'*

Claire (daughter 6)

*'Bed at 8.30, then a DVD, lights off at 10pm. No getting up before 7am, keeping the talking quiet if they do wake up early.'*

Lynsey (sons 9 and 7)

*'At midnight, it's lights out and sleep or everyone goes home. After nine, they're in their room watching a movie or playing quietly. The noise level must be kept to a minimum and they must not make a mess.'*

Sharon (sons 10 and 8)

Whilst a few of our parent panel would allow younger ones a mixed-sex sleepover, by the age of 9 or 10 most would not.

*'At her age, mixed sex doesn't mean much, so if she wanted a boy from school to stay (which I guess is unlikely) I wouldn't mind. We do have boys to stay – we have one set of friends with two sons who quite often stay in L's room. I guess we'll have to review that situation in a few short years!'*

Hollie (daughters 6 and 4)

## What the child psychologist says

Dr Jemma Rosen-Webb:

'It's a very individual decision at what age children are ready for sleepovers. Some are comfortable being away from their parent for the night by the age of 5 or 6, others are still unsure at 8, 9 or older. Sleeping at family members' homes is often a first step and for some children they will have been doing this from a young age anyway. Unless there is a reason you need your child to be able to sleep away from home, be led by them.

If they are older and you think they are missing out on fun with friends, try to work out what might be making them nervous. Do they still wet the bed sometimes? Are they generally anxious being away from you? If you are very worried about it, they may be picking up on your anxieties. If you are having/sending your child to a sleepover, be realistic about how exciting this can be for them and adapt your expectations accordingly about what time they will actually fall asleep!'

## What you can do about it

**Be realistic** Accept the fact they probably won't go to sleep at the normal time.

*'If you want them to go to sleep at a reasonable hour, just don't have a sleepover!'*

Hollie (daughters 6 and 4)

**Be prepared** Have some tricks and strategies to get them to stop nattering and quieten down. Agreeing lights-out time at the outset is a good start. Also having some slightly more calming activities pre-bedtime might help.

*'It's really cheeky but when the younger two have sleepovers, I change the clocks in their bedrooms so it seems an hour later than it is. They think they've stayed up late but they actually go to sleep at a vaguely reasonable time. I daren't do this now with the older one (she has a watch anyway) but the younger two haven't sussed me out yet!'*

Laura (daughters 10 and 8, son 6)

*'I like them to be in bed by 8pm. I expect some chat and giggles. Once it hits 9pm, I start calling up to settle down. If it goes on too late, I make threats that they'll go into separate rooms.'*

Claire (daughter 6)

**Think carefully about limiting numbers** My friend Sue has famous sleepovers for up to 15 kids at a time (they have a big house and clearly even bigger amounts of tolerance and patience – and probably some good ear plugs). For the rest of us a more sensible limit on numbers is advisable!

*'For my elder daughter's eighth birthday party she invited 12 girls from her class to sleepover – we were up all night dealing with them. The last one went to sleep at 5am and the first one was up at 6am. They were tired and grumpy all the next day – even tearful. Now we only allow two children at a time.'*

Heather (daughter 8)

*'I limit it to one child, and they are never allowed friends over to stay at the same time as each other.'*

Amanda (daughter 10, son 8)

**Have a fall-back plan for homesick children** If young children are staying away from home or are at your house for the first time, agree with the other parents what you'll do if they get very homesick, e.g. who is going to get them home if they're hysterical at 2am. Encouraging those prone to mild homesickness to call their parents at bedtime for a quick chat can be an effective pre-emptive measure (although there's a small risk it'll make things worse!).

---

**Tips for successful first sleepovers**

- Don't venture too far from home just in case you have to pick them up at bedtime if they get too upset.
- Choose a familiar family and child for their first ever sleepover.
- No matter how keen they are on the idea, your child probably isn't ready to sleepover elsewhere if they:
  - tend to get clingy at bedtime
  - are still very reliant on a particular routine and don't like deviating from it
  - often wake at night, especially if they want you when this happens.

---

## Further reading

- *Bullying in Britain*, by Adrienne Katz, Ann Buchanan and Victoria Bream, published by Young Voice
- www.beatbullying.org
- www.kidscape.org.uk

# 3

# School and after school

## Homework hassles, school issues and after-school activities

## The big issues

- ✔ Homework haters
- ✔ Helping with homework
- ✔ Testing times: tests and exams
- ✔ Recreational reading
- ✔ After-school activities
- ✔ School refuseniks

Our children's homework can be quite a headache – and not just for them. How many of us feel enthused by explaining long division or patiently going through those spellings for that test yet again after a long day?

In its favour, homework allows you to keep in touch with their classroom life and provides insights into your child's strengths and weaknesses. But on a day-to-day basis, that's scant consolation if you have to nag your homework hater to start and then face frequent yelps for help throughout.

Add test and exam preparation to the after-school hours, plus a smattering of activities (or for some a hectic schedule of everything from extra tuition and drama to sport and piano), and it's a wonder how modern children fit it all in. And what do you do if it's going to school itself rather than what happens afterwards that's the problem?

## Homework haters

Unusual is the child who greets the prospect of homework with unadulterated glee, when the alternatives of, say, the telly or computer (or boiling their own head) are so much more appealing. A few grumbles about homework are very much the norm, but for some, what should be, say, 10 or 15 minutes of work turns into a battle lasting considerably longer.

So how can you make what is often an unappealing aspect of schoolchildren's lives seem at least palatable, and get them getting on with it?

## Background info

- Among the parent panel, 72 per cent report their child is reluctant to do homework at least sometimes.

- Parents tend to take a tougher line as their child progresses through primary school. Many are lenient with younger children, especially if they're tired.

*'We don't always do homework as I don't believe in forcing them at this age if they're particularly tired or not in the mood. Forcing them can be counterproductive. As they get older I will get tougher, though.'*

Suzy (daughter 7, son 4)

- Among the parent panel, 57 per cent refuse television or computer time until homework is done, whilst 26 per cent reward their child for finishing homework.

*'I tell them it has to be done and promise telly time when they've finished. I do also threaten him with telling his teacher he is being uncooperative – that often works.'*

Coralie (sons 7 and 5)

*'I coax every word of [my 6-year-old's] "writing journal" out of him using threats, gentle encouragement and, on occasion, chocolate buttons.'*

Jane (sons 11 and 6)

- Of the panel, 17 per cent have allowed their child to not do their homework (some parents sending the teacher a note explaining the situation). Often this was because parents believe it's more effective for the teacher to respond to it not being done or because these parents don't support the giving of homework at their child's age.

## What the educational expert says

Professor Susan Hallam, author of *Homework: The Evidence*, and Professor of Education at the Institute of Education:

'If a child is reluctant to do homework, offer moral support. Perhaps work alongside them doing some "homework" of your own (anything that involves quiet, concentrated reading or writing). It is not helpful if the rest of the family are undertaking some fun activity, so try to have times when everyone does some "homework".'

## What the child psychologist says

Dr Harriet Tenenbaum:

'Children may not like homework if it is tedious, its relationship to what they are learning is unclear, or there is too much of it. They may also believe that there are more attractive things they could do.

However, research suggests that homework is important for developing good study habits and creating a link between school and home. Whilst it's tempting to use bribes such as saying there will be no TV until they've finished, it's better to try and increase their intrinsic motivation to do it instead.

It is much better to avoid giving the impression that homework is something negative to be endured. Try to explain that homework provides extra practice of skills they've learnt at school, stops them falling behind and helps you know where they're up to. And help them feel proud of their efforts by praising what they've produced. If you really feel that an incentive is the only option, try to keep the link loose – i.e. more "If you finish your homework now, you'll be in time for X [their favourite TV programme]" rather than "You can only watch X if you finish your homework".'

## What you can do about it

**Consider incorporating homework into an after-school routine with a set time** A bit of time off and a brain-fuelling snack beforehand is wise, though. Get to know when your child is usually most receptive and aim for then.

*'She's allowed half an hour rest time after school, so she can get changed, have a snack and chill out. After that it's homework time and, until it's done, TV or distractions are not allowed.'*

Amelia (daughter 10)

*'After school he seems to need a bit of time just playing and watching TV and then for some reason he perks up*

*at about 5.30 just before dinner, so we always do any homework then.'*

Vicki (son 5)

**Alternatively, you might prefer to be flexible and let them choose when it's done** This can make children feel more involved and make it harder for them to try and wangle out of it. Perhaps try both approaches for a week and see which works best.

*'I find it helps to agree in advance when they'll do it. I'll say, "You don't have to do your homework now, but please tell me when you will be doing it". Then they'll say, "At the end of this game" or "Straight after lunch" and then I'll remind them five minutes in advance before they get immersed in something else.'*

Marcia (sons 11, 9 and 6)

**Provide somewhere comfortable, practical and distraction-free** Ideally this will be away from (usually younger) siblings who do not have homework and are playing/watching TV. Some parents choose to sit at the table too and do paperwork/read.

*'I sit at the table with her and get out my own "homework" and we do it together. She reads me her books and makes up funny sentences and I let her "help" me with mine.'*

Angela (daughter 5)

**Provide the stuff they need to get on with it** Take away excuses such as not having the necessary dictionary/ruler/coloured pencils. Work out with them before they start what they need. A fairly firm 'Right, you've got everything, so you can get going' is hard to argue with.

**Offer help, support and praise ... in moderation** (See the section below on helping.) It's not your homework but if a child is overwhelmed or confused they might feel they can't do anything at all. Breaking tasks down into smaller, more approachable steps or helping with the first question might get them going with less fuss. Then praise their efforts.

> 'The middle one gets into such a state that he can't do it. I wait until he's calm, talk it through with him, look at different ways we can approach it and listen to him when he tells me what he thinks he should do.'
>
> Karen (sons 8, 7 and 5)

**Think about whether you want to use incentives** These might include 'No TV/playing until homework is done' – but bear in mind positive rewards often work better. It might not be approved of by all experts but this is the number-one tactic used by our parent panel. Offering to do something fun together afterwards also works for many.

> 'I let him know that is it important to do his homework and acknowledge it positively afterwards, plus I reward him by reminding him he's free to play some games, TV, etc.'
>
> Ivan (son 11)

**Leave it to the teacher to dole out consequences if homework isn't completed** Many children are more motivated by fear of letting down their teacher than they are by wanting not to disappoint their parents. You can always send a note in if you want to explain why it wasn't done.

> *'I tend to take the line that it's their homework – if they don't do it, that's fine, but* they *have to explain to their teacher why it hasn't been done. So far that's worked and it always gets done.'*
>
> Jane (sons 11 and 6)

> *'I have explained that if she does not do homework, she'll have to tell her teacher that she didn't want to do it. This usually does the trick.'*
>
> Allison (daughter 6, son 4)

**Consider letting them stop after a while if it's taking too long or is too difficult** If your child has made a serious effort to do the homework for an appropriate amount of time (you'll have to decide where to draw the line with this), it's reasonable for them to stop, and for you to send a note to the teacher with it along the lines of 'X spent an hour on this but had to stop as it was bedtime/they were stuck', etc. This will help prevent it becoming a battle next time.

> *'If they cannot grasp the concepts after you've explained and demonstrated, then it should go back to school unfinished. It doesn't help them to have homework taken back into school completed by parents – it gives the teacher a false indication of their abilities.'*
>
> Lynsey (sons 9 and 7)

# Helping with homework

*'He asks for help every few questions. I feel like it's my homework too!'*

According to a government website: 'Homework is a fantastic way for you to get more involved in your child's education and find out what they're doing all day.' The implication, then, is you're meant to muck in, but where do you draw the line?

Should you deposit offspring in the furthest corner of the house and run away, offer a little support when asked, or create an entire PhD-standard dissertation and attempt to pass it off as your 8-year-old's own work?

Personally, it's not so much the 3 Rs that I find daunting (well, not at primary-school level anyway), and those obscure questions about goodness knows what rarely remain unsolved after a quick bit of Googling. It's time-consuming 'crafty' projects that I fear the most. Expect me to assist in the construction of papier mâché South American ceremonial warrior swords or run up Book Day outfits and, well, it's not only my enthusiasm that falls apart.

## Background info

- Government guidelines recommend homework should be no more than an hour a week in years 1 and 2, 90 minutes a week in years 3 and 4, and 30 minutes per day in years 5 and 6.

- Research by the publisher Dorling Kindersley with a sample of 1,500 parents of 8–12-year-olds found:

- One in three mums and dads regularly spend up to an hour a week on the internet/reading books to help their children with homework questions.
- 59 per cent admit to sometimes being confused by their child's homework.
- Maths was the subject most likely to leave parents flummoxed, with 48 per cent of them admitting this is their weakest subject.

- There's a huge variation in the amount of homework our parent panel's children get, from none to several hours a week. Most parents in our survey thought their child got about the right amount during term time; however, there were several forceful complaints about homework for weekends and school holidays. A small number of parents objected to their child getting any homework at all.

- There was a correlation between the amount of help given and the age of children. By around age 8 or 9, most parents said they needed to intervene much less than in the first few years of homework being given (although conversely a few parents found they were helping more at this stage if homework was not well matched to their child's ability or was complicated).

*'As my daughter is just learning to read, her homework requires parental presence and support whereas my son does almost all of his solo. Sometimes we check it with him, more for presentation than content. The transition between year 3 and year 4 is very marked in my view; from then on they need to start to learn that mistakes*

*are their own responsibility, so they must check their own work.'*

Marina (son 8, daughter 4)

*'By the time she was 9, I was helping less, just reminding her to do it.'*

Anon (daughter 13, son 9)

## What the educational expert says

Professor Susan Hallam:

> 'It's best to wait until a child directly asks for help or indicates that they're having difficulties. Allow the child to explain the problem in their own terms – teaching methods and the curriculum change very quickly and sometimes the understanding that you have may be inaccurate. If there's a problem, it is a good idea to write a note to the teacher explaining that your child tried to do the homework but did not understand and ask for some guidance to be sent from school. Always remember that it is their homework, *not* yours.'

## What the child psychologist says

Dr Harriet Tenenbaum:

> 'The goal is helping children to understand the material on their own rather than completing the task for them. Children must feel that they understand the work and have mastered the concepts in their homework. Believing that they can complete the assignment can increase their motivation to do it. Watch out for intervening when your child hasn't asked for help; they might find this intrusive rather than helpful and it could make

them feel you're helping because you think they are incapable of doing it alone. This could affect their self-esteem and academic motivation. If you think the homework is regularly too difficult, it's worth going to have a chat with their teacher.'

## What you can do about it

**Help children to help themselves** This is especially important at the older end of the primary age range. Ensure they have the resources to do this, e.g. a dictionary, thesaurus, (supervised) computer access.

> *'I encourage him to find answers to things like what a tricky word means in the dictionary or on the PC, rather than just taking the easy option and asking us.'*
> Alex (son 9)

**Start younger ones off** They might feel daunted or not understand what they've been asked to do.

> *'I read through it with her and ask her to tell me what she thinks she has to do, then when I think she is clear, I leave her to do it by herself but am available for questions if she gets stuck. Then when she has finished one of us will go through what she has done with her and talk about it.'*
> Anita (daughter 6)

**Encourage them to think a little longer before helping with specific questions**

> *'I help her when she asks me to, but much of the time I prefer to encourage her to do things for herself. I say*

*I'm busy at the moment (generally true!) but that I will help later, by which time she has usually come up with a solution for herself.'*

Sara (daughter 8)

**Stay positive and encouraging** Explaining square roots might be the last thing you want to do after a long day but try and see it as a way of keeping in touch with their school life. It's hard, I know, but if you sound bored it won't help them feel enthused by their work.

*'Be encouraging and stay calm. What looks obvious to an adult is often not to a young child. Try not to get frustrated with them – it only makes it worse.'*

Coralie (sons 7 and 5)

**If you feel you're having to help a lot because your child is struggling, talk to their teacher** Find out what the expectations are of how much you should help. Let them know if the homework seems inappropriately difficult.

# Testing times: tests and exams

From that first spelling test via exams such as SATs to, for those applying to selective schools, the 11-plus, everything from revision to results can stress out both children and parents.

A child's personality will have a lot of influence on the way they deal with exams and tests but your own approach can have a big impact too.

## Background info

- Among the parent panel, 47 per cent said their child had been stressed by exams or tests (this excludes those who have yet to sit a test).

- Bribing (sorry: incentivising) older children to do well in tests was reported to be commonplace in the parent panel's schools but only for the 11-plus stage.

*'Loads of 11-year-olds at my son's school get paid for getting good marks. Last year most of the 10-year-olds who took the 11-plus were promised either money or big presents if they passed.'*

Marcia (sons 11, 9 and 6)

## What the child psychologist says

Dr Harriet Tenenbaum:

'Parents need to be careful about putting too much emphasis on tests. Children may lose intrinsic motivation in a subject after a test – even when they do well. It's best if they are taught that effort, skill and strategy are important and that tests do not measure their intelligence or their ability to achieve in the future. It's really important not to make your child feel a failure at this age, even if you feel disappointed by their results.

Teach them that when they receive disappointing results, it does not mean that they are not smart. Discuss whether they put in enough effort or chose a learning strategy that wasn't effective and work out what they could do differently next time.'

## What you can do about it

**Keep things in perspective and don't pressure them**
SATs particularly don't really matter so much in the grand scheme of things. The results don't get put on their college/university application forms and no one will care when they're grown-up. How they do does not represent how good a parent you are either.

> 'Don't stress about SATs – these tests are not important, they will not show on your child's CV.'
>
> Petra (son 8, daughter 5)

> 'For my kids there's a lot of pressure at school, especially for the 11-plus, from other kids as well as from teachers. I think they're getting all the pressure they need, and the teachers' job is to focus on their academic success. Therefore I think my job is to remind them that schoolwork isn't all there is to life, and that happiness doesn't just depend on that.'
>
> Marcia (sons 11, 9 and 6)

**Provide a relaxing environment** If your child is stressed, help them wind down and be there to listen to any worries they have.

> 'A lovely bath the night before with bubbles, a cuddle in bed and lights out after half an hour. Rise a little earlier than normal so the morning is not rushed and then give your child their favourite brekkie: mine prefer porridge and bacon sarnies and plenty of fluids for school.'
>
> Anon (daughter 13, son 9)

*'Home should be a refuge from all that pressure, otherwise where can they go? I'd rather my children were happy and likeable people than academically successful. OK, both would be great, but I think they need a balance. Support the school, sure, but don't add to the stress.'*

Marcia (sons 11, 9 and 6)

**Praise effort as much as results** Children need to hear that it's the trying hard that mattered and that you believe they did their best (if they did try, of course!)

**Give them a treat afterwards** An end-of-exam treat can be a popular way to mark the fact it's all over (well, until next time …).

# Recreational reading

Books are entertainment and education in one. If you're the parent of a reluctant reader, you might not want to hear this but evidence suggests children who enjoy reading do better at school.

Of course, some kids simply aren't bookworms and never will be, but there are plenty who just need a nudge in the right direction – who need their heart setting on fire about reading.

## Background info

Whether the parent panel read to their children or listen to them reading or not varies – as you'd expect, younger children are more often read to than older ones who can manage on their own better. Our parent panel typically stopped reading to their children regularly once they were confident readers, although a few continued.

> *'I still read to my 9-year-old because he loves it, although after I go downstairs he'll read maybe 150 pages to himself. My oldest, however, stopped wanting to be read to by the time he was 8.'*
>
> Marcia sons (11, 9 and 6)

> *'I only read with them occasionally as they are both good readers. They sometimes ask about words or come and read something interesting to me. I read to them about once a week.'*
>
> Sharon (sons 10 and 8)

## What the child psychologist says

Dr Harriet Tenenbaum:

'Parental modelling of book reading is very important. Children in homes where parents read and own lots of books are more likely to want to read. For this reason, it might be good to have a regular time set aside where everyone (adults included) reads. Children can find reading off-putting if they think they won't understand some of the words, so it's worth quickly skimming a book to highlight any words with which your children may experience difficulty.

Studies suggest gender differences, with girls reporting reading more than boys do. If you've got a reluctant boy reader, he might like comic books or scary stories. Remember too that books are not the only type of reading that can improve reading skills. If a child loves football, they could, for example, read a magazine geared to football or the scores in the newspaper.'

## What you can do about it

**Tap into their interests** There are children's books about everything these days, from football to cookery. If you can start with these to engender an enthusiasm for reading, you can then move on to other topics once they've hopefully caught the book bug. Don't neglect non-fiction. Hook them into a series or a particular author and then look for similar reads.

**Find a local or online children's book club** Many libraries have these or search online. Storytelling sessions or going to a reading by a favourite author at a bookshop might help – then get them to choose some other books to read afterwards.

**Don't worry too much if a book for recreational reading doesn't have challenging vocabulary** Just encourage them to read per se at first. Similarly, if they like reading the same book again and again, that's fine too.

> 'I'd rather he read lots of different books but he seems drawn to the same two or three – I'm happy that he's reading at all, though.'
>
> Vicki (son 5)

**Try something completely different** Silly poetry perhaps. If they've never got into fiction, try non-fiction. Even a joke book might just get them turning pages.

**Get creative** Tackle a story-inspired project in the holidays or at the weekend – then introduce the book. It might be a trip to an Alice in Wonderland ride at a theme park or anything which will appeal to your child and which there's a book to tie in with. Film–book tie-ins can also help reluctant readers to pick up books – if they've seen a film and enjoyed it, head to the bookshop/library afterwards.

> '*He loved the film* Charlie and the Chocolate Factory, *so after that I bought the book and then we moved on to some other Roald Dahls. It helped him get into the habit of reading and realising it could be fun and not just about boring school reading scheme books.*'
>
> Mel (sons 8 and 6)

**Talk about books you and they are reading** Ask them questions about it, e.g. about what they do and don't like, who their favourite character is, which character they'd like to be in the book (but don't turn it into the Spanish Inquisition).

**Perhaps offer an extra book allowance on top of pocket money** If you can afford it, there's nothing like a bit of extra cash to motivate some kids. A fiver a fortnight to buy a book of their choice on a regular trip to the bookshop might just grab their attention. Then you have to hope they actually read it, of course.

**Provide a special shelf or box for them to keep their books in** Some kids will also like to add book plates with their name or a nice bookmark. None of this is going to magically transform a really reluctant reader but it will add a sense of ownership and involvement with their books.

**Some other tricks ...** Build a (dark) den and send them in there with books and a torch. If you're reading together and your child is the physical type, create actions for particular words that are repeated a lot – so for younger children every time the word cat is mentioned, they have to miaow; if the story involves flying, they have to pretend to fly, etc.

**Read together** Attention-hungry kids will appreciate the one-on-one time. If they're desperate to know what happens next in a chapter book, you might just find them picking it up themselves later on.

# After-school activities

Where once a weekly session at Brownies or Cubs sufficed, now there's a whole industry of after-school activities, from drama via ballroom dancing to extra maths.

But how many children really have diaries as packed as the average A-list *Hello!* magazine socialite or is all this a bit of an urban myth? In fact, urban might be the operative word here as there's certainly a perception that being ferried from ballet to Brownies and back again is a bit of a middle-class metropolitan phenomenon.

Are you short-changing your child if their post-school time consists of nothing more than a spot of TV, a snack and some plain old-fashioned playtime, rather than a round of 'enrichment' activities? Or is over-scheduling more detrimental to their development, leaving them with little idea of how to entertain themselves?

## Background info

- Among the parent panel's children, 11 per cent do no extra-curricular activities, 38 per cent do one to two hours a week (during term time), 33 per cent do two to four hours a week and 18 per cent do more than four hours. Amounts tend to increase as children get older.

*'The oldest two do four hours a week, A does football and swimming for two hours.'*

Sue (daughters 10 and 8, son 5)

*'A, my 10-year-old, does seven hours of kung fu, Cubs, drumming and French, S does four hours of kung fu, Cubs and swimming.'*

Sharon (sons 10 and 8)

- TheBabyWebsite.com commissioned a survey of 3,000 parents about extra-curricular activities in 2009. The top five activities by the proportion of kids doing them were:

1. Swimming (38 per cent).
2. Football (25 per cent).
3. Brownies/Cubs/Guides/Scouts (15 per cent).
4. Music lessons (15 per cent).
5. Dance (15 per cent).

## What the child psychologist says

Dr Harriet Tenenbaum:

'Research suggests extra-curricular activities are related to improvements in children's confidence and academic achievement. However, it is important not to over-schedule children because they need time to play and be spontaneous too. Spontaneous play helps children learn how to self-regulate their emotions and wishes, increases their imagination, contributes to their cognitive development, and helps them learn how to act in different situations with a variety of different people.'

## What you can do about it

**Watch out for over-scheduling** As our psychologist says above, children need downtime and unstructured play at home and with their friends. So, although extra-curricular activities can be fantastic, remember they already spend about 30 to 32 hours a week at school and might have another couple of hours of homework on top of this. Adding another five for activities makes that as much as many adults' working hours. It's all about balance!

**Don't feel like there's a competition to provide your child with as many skills as possible** If your child is tired enough after a day at school and prefers to simply catch up with their favourite toys at home, stick with that and try not to feel they're missing out. A busy schedule of after-school dance and drama classes might create an all-singing, all-dancing child but it won't necessarily make them happier. You are not failing your child if they don't do Mandarin classes, violin, etc. by age 7! Especially if they'd be too exhausted to enjoy it all anyway.

**Stand firm** If they have different ideas each week about what activities they want to do or they want to do too much, it's perfectly reasonable to limit them to two or three activities a week.

*'I will not force them to do anything. (I remember hating music lessons.) With any opportunities for clubs/classes, we let them make the choice to go. Once they have decided, they must stick with their decision for the duration.'*

Trudi (daughter 9, son 7)

# School refuseniks

Not all children skip happily through the school gate. School is a massive part of their lives and if they don't like going, for whatever reason, it can be extremely difficult all round.

There are tons of reasons for a child not wanting to go to school – bullying, boredom, changes in their lives making them feel insecure – and sometimes no apparent reason at all.

## Background info

Just over a quarter of the parent panel's children had had a phase of not wanting to go to school (more than just a very occasional day or a quick grumble here or there).

## What the expert says

Antonia Chitty, author of *What to Do When Your Child Hates School*:

'If your child has always gone to school happily, it can be a real problem when suddenly they start to object to going. Primary-school-age children may not always be able to explain what the problem is either, so you need to do a bit of detective work to find out. Some children will tell you that they dislike school, while others bottle it up inside. There are signs that show if your child is secretly stressed and many children make their dislike of school evident by apparent "bad behaviour". They may be actively disruptive and unable to sit still, or easily distracted and dream instead of doing what they are asked. This range of behaviour can indicate one of a number of problems – speak to your child's teacher and the school's special needs coordinator (SENCO) if these are a concern. Other causes of disliking going to school include bullying and events in their home life such as a bereavement or divorce.'

## What you can do about it

**It might just be a short phase, so don't react too much initially** Lots of children have a few days when they're not too keen on the idea of school. Sometimes for no serious reason. You might just ride it out without too much fuss and by not overreacting will prevent it turning into a more sustained problem.

*'We had a phase when both of them were complaining about going to school every day. It was tiresome and I had to chivvy them along a lot each morning. I don't know what was going on but it stopped after a few days of me standing firm and insisting they had to go.'*

Sangeeta (twin sons, 7)

**If the problem is acute or persists, try and ascertain the underlying cause** Work on getting your child to open up when it's not a 'heat of the moment' time. So not when you're late for school and they're in tears. If they won't talk to you about it, perhaps they will with someone else – grandparents, an aunt or uncle or favourite babysitter?

Common reasons to look out for include bullying/friendship issues, boredom, learning difficulties and a poor relationship with a teacher. A child who has a hearing or sight problem might also find school less enjoyable.

**Speak to the teacher** Find out what seems to be going on in school, especially if there's evidence of bullying – a key cause of school hating (see page 20 for more advice on this).

*'I started kicking up a massive fuss each morning and sometimes would be crying at bedtime about how she didn't want to go in the next day. I couldn't get out of her what was going on for a while – although I knew it was about friends. I managed to piece together more when I'd spoken to the teacher.'*

Deb (daughter 8)

**Keep a dialogue open** If something major has happened in your child's home life, such as divorce or bereavement, keep a dialogue open with the teacher. This way they can provide any extra reassurance or support for your child. You will also need to reassure them yourself that you/another carer will be there when they get home/to pick them up.

**Watch out for fake illnesses** These are one of the most common signs of not wanting to go to school in children this age. Annoyingly it can be hard to know when they're crying wolf and when they're really ill. Nine times out of ten, threatening a trip to the doctors will get illness fibbers to confess that they were making it up or make them miraculously better in seconds.

> *'Some days it was obvious she was trying it on with fake tummy aches but other times I didn't know whether she really was ill. I started calling the GP to book an appointment and very quickly her "stomach ache" resolved.'*
>
> Deb (daughter, 8)

## Further reading

- *What to Do When Your Child Hates School*, by Antonia Chitty, published by White Ladder Press

# 4
# Food, glorious food

**There's nothing quite like it ... for creating a mealtime argument**

# The big issues

- ✔ Mealtime manners
- ✔ Fussy eaters
- ✔ Weight worries
- ✔ Junior vegetarians
- ✔ Snacks and junk

Those little urchins in the musical *Oliver* sang about the gloriousness of food and their eagerness to get their mitts on anything edible. Fast forward to 21st-century real life and the side effect of food in abundance is that the average British child is less ravenous and certainly not crying out for pease pudding and saveloys (actually I don't blame them for that – they don't exactly sound appetising). Vegetables are often viewed with suspicion rather than eaten with grateful gusto. And persuading them to try anything new can be as challenging as getting the Artful Dodger on to the straight and narrow.

Add to this the nagging (you) about table manners, the nagging (them) for junk and worries about obesity at one end of the scale and eating disorders at the other, and it's unsurprising that many parents feel there's a battle going on across the family dining table. That is, if there still is a family dining table and it's not all TV dinners.

## Mealtime manners

*'Trying to get them to slow down, chew properly, eat with cutlery not fingers ... all these things are big issues*

*here. I'm constantly saying "You've got too much in your mouth" and "Use your fork".'*

The average primary-school child would, without us going on at them, likely eat with the refinement of a ravenous Stone Age caveman (cavechild?). So it falls upon us, their parents, to 'table train' them.

It's a personal thing as to how far you want to go with this – some want to create kids akin to finishing school graduates (indeed, my own mum really is a finishing school graduate and still gets apoplectic if one of us shovels with a wrong-way-up fork or commits similar crimes against etiquette). Others are satisfied if their offspring know sufficient basics to avoid embarrassment over Sunday lunch at Great Aunt Doris's.

## Background info

- According to 95 per cent of adults surveyed by YouGov (commissioned by food maker Birds Eye), table manners still matter. That said, 40 per cent believe they're more relaxed about table manners than their own parents were, 84 per cent discourage talking with mouths full but only 54 per cent believe cutlery should be held properly.

- Our parent panel view the following as required 'basic' manners for their primary-school-age children:

    - Using cutlery rather than fingers (with reasonable exceptions such as burgers).

    - Chewing with a closed rather than gaping open mouth and not talking with a mouth full of food.

    - Eating in a measured way, e.g. no licking plates, slurping noises, taking ridiculously big chomps/

over-filling mouths, burping (or at least apologising if this really couldn't be avoided).

- Being polite about any food they don't like, especially at other people's houses, so no 'Yuck that tastes like pigeon poo' comments about the aforementioned Great Aunt Doris's 'culinary delights'.

- Sitting down 'properly', e.g. no feet on tables, and not leaving the table for trivial reasons halfway through meals.

- No toys or games at the table at home (the vast majority were allowed them in restaurants).

- Staying at the table until everyone has finished (a few parents are fine about early departures as long as their child asks to get down).

- Some rules common among our own parents' generation have largely been dropped, e.g. not putting elbows on the table and saying thank you when things are passed are viewed as either only essential in a small minority of families or as 'nice-to-haves' by the majority.

- The parent panel aren't too worried about 'correct' use of cutlery by younger children (most said they let it go if their 5-year-old wasn't holding a knife and fork perfectly as long as they were using them).

## What the child psychologist says

Dr Jemma Rosen-Webb:

'Children learn through watching and copying. Initially this is from their parents and, later on, other children. Think about what your child sees you do – if you pick your favourite parts out of the salad, you can't expect them not to do the same! Making sure you have meals with your children at least some of the time gives them opportunities to learn the way you like things done, e.g. asking them to pass something rather than leaning across and taking it (if that's important to you).

Children have to learn to adapt their behaviour to different situations (home, school, friend's house), based on what the expectations of that situation are. This may take some time and they might try things that are allowed in one place and see if they can "get away with them" in another.

Finally, think about what's fair to expect of your child based not only on their age but also their ability. For example, some children find using cutlery much harder than others. Adapt expectations accordingly and remember that it takes a long time to learn new skills.'

## What the etiquette expert says

Sean Davoren, Head Butler at London's Lanesborough Hotel, author of *Manners from Heaven* – a guide to improving children's etiquette:

'Showing your children how to hold a knife and fork will stand them in good stead in the future. Manners are respect for the people around you – they're important because we are all judged by everyone we meet. You may not always be remembered for your good manners but you will be remembered for your bad manners! And remember, children are led by example.'

## What you can do about it

**Prioritise** Decide which manners really matter to you, explain why and stop nagging about the others.

> 'I've found if I go on too much about all the little things and expect perfection we all just get frustrated. I'm only working on the really important stuff for now.'
>
> Karen (son 6)

**Set a good example, eating together where possible** Watch your own manners – if you always pick up chips with your fingers at home/talk with your mouth full, guess what your kids are probably going to start doing?

**Help them recognise when they need to be on 'best behaviour'** Most adults relax manners a little at home but could raise their game should they ever dine with, say, the Queen. Teaching your children to know when to turn on their finest etiquette means you can ease off on the nagging somewhat at home.

> 'She's learnt now when it's time for best behaviour and when it's OK to let her guard down. It keeps things more relaxed when it's just the three of us, but she knows the "right" way to eat in front of my mother-in-law.'
>
> Amy (daughter 10)

**Use role playing or a special dinner to bring in new rules** This can be much more effective and breaks the cycle of you nagging them.

*'A couple of times we've done a special meal as a way to introduce better table manners. One time we went to a nice restaurant and made out it was a big, grown-up treat but they had to eat properly, and we brought in a couple of new rules then.'*

Nick (sons 9 and 6)

**Accept that restaurant meals might require different rules** Notably about toys and crayons at the table. Have realistic expectations if there'll be a long wait for the meal or between courses.

*'In restaurants I'm quite happy for her to do some colouring if we go somewhere where crayons are doled out. If there aren't any, I have an armoury of games like I-spy or we make up stories whilst we wait for the food.'*

Victoria (daughter 9)

## Fussy eaters

*'One of them will say 'I don't like it' and then the other starts copying, even with something they liked the week before.'*

Faddy eating is one of the biggest issues with this age group. According to child psychologists, some fussiness is normal for children and indeed could actually be a smart (if irritating for you) survival strategy – they avoid new foods because the unknown might be harmful.

Another theory is that faddy eaters have more sensitive taste buds than others, making them less open to trying new foods or accepting stronger flavours. Note: do not tell your children this, or every time they will abdicate responsibility for refusing veg by declaring it all their tastebuds' fault.

Fussy tastebuds, survival instinct or otherwise, there is still plenty you can try to get them to give peas a chance (or whatever it is they object to). 'Try' is the operative word, I'm afraid – you can employ every tactic going but a hardened fusser might still stubbornly refuse anything beyond a very narrow range of foods, no matter what you do.

Reassuringly, this is rarely a major health issue, and as you're scraping most of that lovingly made meal in the bin for the fifth time this week, remember that few 20-year-olds survive solely on jam sandwiches/plain pasta with no sauce/whatever other quirky idea of a balanced diet your child currently has.

## Background info

- Just under a third of our parent panel's children were described by their parents as fussy eaters.

- Most had got neither better nor worse since starting school – only a very small minority had been influenced by peer pressure in the dinner hall.

*'She used to eat everything put in front of her until she started school. Now she copies her friends and has started refusing carrots, peas and other food – because her friends don't like them!'*

Anon (daughter 5)

- Among the parent panel, 72 per cent actually reported their children like eating vegetables, which goes against the idea that seems to prevail in the media that all children hate veg!

- Meanwhile, 69 per cent of the parent panel give their child nothing else if they don't like what they've made for a meal, 21.5 per cent let them have something else but only something very limited, e.g. bread and butter, or cereal, and another 9.5 per cent make their child an alternative meal if this happens.

- Around half do involve them in choosing what's going to be dished up, albeit usually from limited options (e.g. 'Do you want lasagne or fishcakes tonight?' rather than giving them free rein).

- Even though it's not recommended by experts (see below), some of our parent panel do bribe with pudding.

*'Five mouthfuls of veg earns you a nice pudding.'*

Jo (daughter 4)

*'I usually give them two different veg and get them to eat at least half before they get pudding.'*

Trudi (daughter 9, son 7)

- Research by University College, London, found that the foods 4–5-year-olds hate the most include avocado, leeks, cottage cheese, sweet pepper, onion, liver, cabbage and marrow (I'm with them on the last three).

## What the nutritionist says

Sally Child, author of *Dealing with Difficult Eaters*:

'Try to only give praise, not punishment, and don't compare them with a sibling or friend who eats well – this doesn't really work. Respect that they may dislike some things or not be hungry every meal or every day. If they refuse to eat a meal, don't offer anything else until the next scheduled snack or meal and quietly remove the leftover food (you can scream later!).

Offering limited choices within a healthy range, e.g. "Do you want beans or tuna on your jacket potato?" works well. Cooking and eating together also helps. Don't be tempted to give them anything to eat just to "get something into them". Every mouthful should count and be healthy, especially if they have a small appetite. Finally, make sure they do not have a medical reason for poor eating. If you suspect one, seek further advice.'

## What the child psychologist says

Dr Jemma Rosen-Webb:

'In trying to understand your child's fussy eating, it may be helpful to think right back to their earliest feeding experiences. Where did things start to go wrong? Also, what is your own relationship with food like? Have you got into a negative cycle of both feeling very stressed around mealtimes? Children are very sensitive to parents' emotional states. If you are stressed and worried, they might be too and will find it harder to eat. Try to relax and stay calm. Mealtimes should be relaxed, fun and enjoyable.

Try to think from your child's perspective too. It's natural to be wary of new foods. Even adults can be hesitant when offered a food they don't recognise. Keep the focus on the positive, e.g. how grown-up they are to try some potato. You may also want to try playfully challenging them to eat more of a food you know they at least moderately like: "How many green beans can you eat?"

Never force your child to eat something or you risk giving food negative connotations, which can end up in a battle of wills.

Let your child become familiar with food in a non-threatening way. Ask them if they want to help with food preparation. The more they are used to touching and smelling different foods, the more likely they are to try them. Some people are more sensitive to textures than others and if that is the case then touching different foods may help them to get used to new textures.

Think about the way you talk about different foods too and how this may influence your child's view of them. If you always offer dessert as a reward for eating vegetables, vegetables may become a necessary evil in order to get the good stuff. This makes desserts seem more desirable and vegetables less desirable.

Seek advice from a medical practitioner if you're worried that your child is not gaining weight, is losing weight or is substantially missing out on important vitamins or minerals. They will either be able to reassure you or refer you on for more specific help.'

## What you can do about it

**Don't plead or cajole** Saying 'Just try it' is the surest way to ensure some children just won't.

*'Never give the impression that you really want them to try something or you might just meet their rebellious side. If you don't make too much fuss they will usually try it eventually.'*

Marian (stepdaughter 7, son 5)

**Never force them to try something new** It doesn't help solve their underlying aversion to new foods and just turns mealtimes into a battle.

**Instead encourage and even employ a bit of trickery** Talk positively about the food concerned – perhaps eat it yourself and make a point about how delicious/healthy it is, etc. My mum reminding us that Popeye's favourite food was spinach worked a treat when I was a child (well, with my brothers at least – I was less keen on the bulging biceps idea).

*'He still loves to be seen to be older than he is, so sometimes I tell him a particular food is really quite grown-up, and it definitely gets him trying it out.'*

Susan (son 6)

*'If they make a fuss about broccoli we say "OK then, you can have sprouts instead" – they usually then agree that broccoli is the lesser of two evils!'*

Georgia (daughter 9, son 7)

*'Clock which playmates eat broccoli and invite them over lots!'*

Kate (son 8, daughter 4)

**Remind them that they had to try everything once** This is true even of their favourite foods and they can't claim they dislike something if it's never even passed their lips. A gentle 'But if you'd never tried ice cream, how would you ever know you liked that?' and the like can work well. Once they do try something, pile on the praise even if they don't like it.

> 'I remind them that they had to try everything they eat already to see if they liked it … if they hadn't they'd have missed out on their favourites.'
>
> Eve (daughter 9, son 6)

> 'We have always used the principle of "You can't say you don't like it unless we see you try it". Most of the time they like it.'
>
> Anita (daughters 6 and 4)

**Let them know there's no pressure if they genuinely don't like it** It's literally a lot more palatable for a child to think about one mouthful than having to eat a whole pile of something they might dislike.

> 'We have a one-spoon rule. They have to try one spoon, if they genuinely don't like it, I won't force it.'
>
> Elaine (sons 6 and 5)

**Involve them in what's being dished up** Get your offspring to lend a hand with cooking, growing veg, and/or picking meals from a small selection.

> 'In the morning I ask what he would like for his tea – I've found it helps for him to feel he's choosing (when in fact I'm steering him towards the things he can choose).'
>
> Frankie (son, 4)

*'We get a local seasonal veg box and the kids really love seeing what's turned up each week. It helps them be more enthusiastic about veg.'*

Sharon (sons 10 and 8)

*'I allow them to veto one food item each from the family menu (this is quite funny – my 9- and 6-year-olds stupidly vetoed the same thing).'*

Marcia (sons 11, 9 and 6)

**Highlight when a new food is similar to something they like** So meatballs are just little round burgers, sweet potato wedges are different-shaped, orange-coloured chips, etc.

*'With a new recipe try to make it similar to one they will eat and push the parts of it they really like. My kids will eat rice with chicken and tomato sauce; I got them to eat curry by telling them it was rice with chicken and tomato sauce with a couple of other ingredients.'*

Adrian (daughter 6)

*'If they ask what something is, it helps to present the food as similar to something else they normally eat: "It's a black eye bean – a bit like those butter beans you like".'*

Marian (stepdaughter 7, son 5)

*'I find it best to introduce new elements into a liked dish rather than to present children with a completely new meal.'*

Jon (childminder)

**Make new foods fun** Kids adore dipping and dunking their nosh (even when they're not meant to). Let them dip fruit into molten chocolate (you don't need a fondue set – just melt the chocolate in the microwave in little bowls), or pour their own sauce over food themselves rather than serving it up 'done'.

*'If I give mine cauliflower cheese they turn their nose up at it, but they love vegetable chunks to dip in their own personal bowl of cheese sauce.'*

Marcia (sons 11, 9 and 6)

*'We make a game of it with different foods set out in bowls to try. Maybe with a theme such as foods from a certain country. Or we do blindfolded tastings with some firm favourites in there so they're willing to keep trying.'*

Suzy (daughter 7, son 4)

**Don't give up** Wait a while and offer it again rather than assuming they just don't like it. Or if you can bear the waste, keep including whatever it is in family meals in small amounts until you wear their resistance down. One day they might just surprise you.

*'Keep trying – my daughter was a curry refusenik until a few months ago.'*

Kate (daughter 8, son 4)

**Use restaurant meals as an opportunity to introduce new things** Encourage them to try a mouthful or two of your meal (the danger of doing this is that they like it too much, leaving you with their plate of chicken nuggets instead). Buffet restaurants are particularly fantastic for bringing a bit of something different to their plates.

**Try to not offer alternatives if a meal is rejected** It's hard to leave them not having eaten but children this age will be OK. By dishing up something else you're giving a message that it's OK to pick and choose whenever they want.

*'If they don't eat it, then they don't get anything else. Sometimes if it's not one of M's favourite dishes but still something she likes, then she'll just have a couple of mouthfuls and say she's full but then five minutes later be saying she's hungry and asking for something else, so this rule is aimed at her really.'*

Suze (daughter 7, son 4)

**Hide your frustration** Do your best to act like you don't care whether they eat what you've made, even if you've spent hours lovingly making it. This is especially important if you suspect food has become a bit of a power struggle.

*'If she doesn't eat a meal, I duck behind the kitchen counter, ram my fist in my mouth, gently remind her to eat and then calmly throw the food away at the end of the meal. Pressuring her to eat could make a fairly neutral issue into an emotional minefield.'*

Issy (daughters 7 and 5)

*'Don't make it a battle – it's better to just take the plate away and get rid of the tension. Someone also said to me once that you should consider your child's diet over a week, not a day – so as long as they're getting a good balance of all the food groups and nutrients over seven days, they probably won't go far wrong – even if on one particular day it's all cheese and yoghurt!'*

Jo (daughter 4)

**Don't slave over a hot stove** There's no point slaving away for two hours over a dish that is unlikely to appeal to your children. Remember, one of the many laws of parenting is that the likelihood of a child eating a meal is inversely proportionate to the effort put into preparing it.

**Remain realistic** Few adults like all foods, so surely children shouldn't fairly be expected to eat anything and everything?

**Try not to bribe** We know it can be effective for some kids (and plenty of our parent panel do it) but try not to bribe them to eat something they don't want to with the promise of pudding. It really does send the message that the pud is covetable and the main course somehow inferior. Keep puddings separate from whether the main course is eaten unless your child is holding off eating their main course and waiting for dessert.

**Only cook one meal** It's fine to have variations on a theme, e.g. if you're happy with one child having pasta with grated cheese only and another having it with sauce, but try to avoid cooking different meals for different children. Your children's eating habits might lead you to swear as much as Gordon Ramsay but *you* are not running a restaurant!

# Weight worries

*'She's only 9 but, despite being slim, already talks about watching her weight all the time.'*

As a tubby 1980s kid, my extra pounds were attributed to puppy fat (rather than the three chocolate digestives and packet of crisps I consumed daily after school) and, rightly or wrongly, no one in the family thought much about it. There was considerably less media coverage of both the dangers of being overweight and of those annoyingly skinny celebs who can give even the scrawniest beanpole pre-teen a complex.

It would be lovely to think today's children could enjoy a childhood as immune as mine was from worrying about being too fat or too thin (there's plenty of time for that in adulthood after all – I know I've made up for it since). But, like it or not, increasing numbers of overweight kids, sedentary lifestyles and the size-zero debate have made weight a big issue for parents and children alike.

And with, on the one hand, this growing pressure to be thin and at the other end of the scale (or should that be scales?) an obesity 'epidemic', it can be hard to know what to do and say as a parent without giving your kids a complex.

## Background info

- Eating disorders are actually rare in under-13s – there are only around 200 reported cases a year in this age group in the UK.

- Our parents panel's experience backs this up. Although quite a few were concerned that their child was underweight, no one had encountered proper eating disorders in this age group.

- The government's national child measurement programme reports that almost a quarter of 4- and

5-year-olds are now overweight or obese. By year 6, nearly a third are.

- No one on the parent panel had actually told their child that they were putting them on a diet but 5 per cent had decided to introduce a programme of healthier eating due to concerns that their child was overweight, and a similar number had introduced higher-fat foods due to their child seeming too thin.

## What the child psychologist says

Dr Jemma Rosen-Webb:

'Our perceptions of "overweight" have changed over the past few decades and we tend to misjudge, perhaps thinking that kids are a healthy weight when they are actually overweight, or worrying that they're underweight when they're not. If you're concerned about your child's weight, talk to a health practitioner – they will be able to advise you or refer you to a more specialist service.

Discuss eating healthily with your kids rather than dieting, and include the importance of exercise. Again, try to notice and praise what they are already doing, to build on it, e.g. "You are great at running and that's really good for your heart" or "It's fantastic that you love milk in the morning because it makes your teeth and bones really strong".

Encourage them to eat regularly: if we skip meals, we're more likely to eat greater quantities and higher-calorie foods when we next eat. If they're overeating, think about how your child is feeling in general and what the triggers might be. Are they using food to console themselves after having a difficult day at school? Can you help them find other comfort or ways to talk about what's troubling them?

Research also tells us that we eat more if we are not paying attention to our food, e.g. while we are watching TV. If this is the case, you may want to limit the places that your family eats, e.g. having a rule that you always eat at a table.

Finally, think about what you are modelling for your child. Healthy eating and good exercise habits need to be worked on as a family. It can be genuinely good fun to exercise together, e.g. going for a walk or a bike ride, and if it's fun everyone is more likely to want to do it again.'

## What you can do about it

**Avoid discussing your own weight anxieties** Some of us make remarks about the size of our rears/tummies/bingo wings (or, if you're like me, all three). But these seemingly harmless comments could affect your child's self-image, so be careful about what you're saying in front of them.

> 'I used to make comments all the time about being too fat, my fat bits, etc. but I've now realised I'm really not setting a good example to my daughters by doing this. My mum used to do it all the time and I'm sure it's at the heart of some of my body hang-ups.'
>
> Laura (daughters 10 and 8, son 6)

**Monitor your children's weight** But not so often that it becomes an obsession. There's really no need to be weighing a child without a known weight problem every day or week.

**Subtly introduce healthier eating rather than officially declaring them on a diet** Likewise, covertly introduce more calorie-rich food for children who are underweight – making them aware is fine, making a big issue could create anxiety.

> '[When they needed to lose weight] I didn't tell them, I just reduced portion sizes and changed cooking methods and types of food.'
>
> Amanda (daughter 10, son 8)

> 'When one of the girls was underweight, we had an "Every mouthful counts" strategy – small amounts of high-calorie food. So "eggy bread" or porridge made with cream rather than cereal for breakfast, cheese as a snack, old-fashioned puddings.'
>
> Issy (daughters 7 and 5)

**Provide gentle reassurance about unwarranted body image concerns** It's hard for children to avoid the pressure to be thin these days but you can reassure them they don't need to worry. Highlight other non-physical characteristics so they don't focus so much on appearance.

> 'My daughter did have a bit of upset when a girl in her class called her fat a few times. We talked about how ridiculous that was and how anyway, even if she had have been fat, it was none of this other girl's business!'
>
> Vic (daughter, 6)

## Junior vegetarians

'My son was completely horrified when, aged 5, he discovered that burgers and bolognaise had "dead cows"

*in them. He was very upset and stopped eating meat.*
*When he was about 6, he stopped eating fish too, declaring*
*tearfully one mealtime when I had bought fish and chips*
*as a treat "I might as well be eating Daddy's goldfish".'*

A few young children, on getting wind of the fact that
meat and fish are actually dead animals rather than
something that magically appears upon Tesco's shelves,
decide to go vegetarian. This can be problematic for meat-
eating families – you might have worries about having to
cook two different meals or ensuring your child obtains
necessary nutrients from a meat-free diet, especially if you
aren't used to considering this.

Conversely when children from vegetarian families start
school they sometimes want to eat meat. If they demand
pepperoni on their pizza, it can feel like a rejection of your
own values. Apart from the dietary suggestions, much of
the advice below applies the other way round to veggies
who've turned carnivore.

## Background info

- Data from the Vegetarian Society suggests 3 per cent
  of 4–11-year-olds are vegetarian and a further 2 per
  cent do not eat meat but do eat fish.

- Only a handful of our parent panel's children had
  gone against the family diet by declaring themselves
  veggie/carnivorous or not sticking with their parents'
  cultural or religious food-related rules.

## What the nutritionist says

Sally Child:

> 'Sudden changes in eating habits are quite common in primary-school children. They are subject to peer influences, might see vegetarianism as a new and sophisticated way of eating or become more aware of animal rights issues and choose not to eat little chickens or lambs.
>
> You need to respect their wishes whilst educating them on both sides of the story. Try not to force your own views on them. This is part of growing up and they need to know they can make choices. Vegetarianism is not a health hazard, but you may need to learn a bit about how to do it properly. Many convenience foods such as veggie sausages or burgers can be high in fat and not very healthy.
>
> Nutrients most likely to be in short supply for vegetarians are iron and protein but vegetarians who eat dairy products should get enough calcium and vitamin D. Increase foods such as pulses, beans, nuts and seeds if they are not allergic. Some schools do not allow nuts due to the few who may have a serious allergy, so you may need to give these at home. Quorn is a good low-fat option for replacing protein, and iron is found in fresh green vegetables and lentils, which can be hidden in stews and soups. Quite often after a short while on the alternatives, a young child will change their mind and should be praised for their efforts and allowed to back-track without feeling they have failed.'

## What the child psychologist says

Dr Jemma Rosen-Webb:

'Try to think of any deviations from the family norm as your child experimenting and working out who they are as an individual. Breaking of strong family values or religious rules about food can be particularly difficult as a parent but try to stay calm and explain to them why you have those rules. Find out what their point of view is. Is it an ethical stand? Are they worried about seeming different from other children at school? Try to come up with solutions together as to how you will manage the change.'

## What you can do about it

**Take views seriously** Find out why a child wants to change their diet and discuss the pros and cons. If they firmly refuse to eat animal products, there isn't going to be a lot you can do about it, so you'd better get used to adding Quorn and tofu to the family shopping list for the foreseeable.

> *'My son became a veggie for about two days. We talked as a family about good, humane farming practices and buy meat only from free-range/organic sources.'*
>
> Kate (son 8, daughter 5)

**Let them try their new diet without making a big issue out of it** They might change their mind pretty quickly anyway.

> *'My eldest was vegetarian for about five minutes when he was 8. I'm afraid I pretended to be supportive, then made bacon butties for lunch – hence it only lasting five minutes. If either of them wants to be veggie when they are older, that would be fine.'*
>
> Jane (sons 11 and 6)

**If they persist, educate them about the pros and cons of their choice** If they are a carnivorous convert, explain the ways they can avoid too much animal fat in their diet. If your child is determined to be a veggie, help them learn about ensuring their diet stays healthy, with plenty of protein.

**Get your child to lend a helping hand with any extra work caused by their decision** It's a good opportunity to involve them in menu planning, shopping and cooking. Work out where you, they and the rest of the family are willing to compromise. If they want to eat meat and you are a veggie family, perhaps agree they can do so outside the home.

## Snacks and junk

*'They have become more prone to peer pressure about eating sweets and junk food and I am always being told what their friends are allowed to eat and how unfair I am for not allowing sweets every day of the week!'*

Most of us recognise a little bit of what you fancy doesn't do much harm, and scoffing a fabulously yummy cake or pack of sweets is surely one of the delights of childhood. But getting the balance right can be tricky, especially when faced with birthday-party teas brimming with goodies, sweet-wielding grandparents and the like.

The lure of processed and child-oriented food can also be an issue and sometimes linked to fussy eating. Many children will turn their nose up at a 'proper' piece of cheese when presented with one specifically marketed to kids, with colourful packaging and quite bold marketing messages.

## Background info

- Fizzy drinks – and especially cola – are almost universally banned at home for the under-8s among our parent panel's children. Conversely, older children tend to be allowed some cola or similar but mainly only at parties/ special occasions. This mum's view was pretty typical:

   *'Cola is not allowed. They have had the occasional sip of mine (I'm a hypocrite!) or a finger in a bottom of their cup but I don't let them have a whole glassful. They have enough energy already without giving them caffeine!'*

   Suzy (daughter 7, son 4)

- The foods most commonly banned by the parent panel were:
   - products containing artificial sweeteners
   - cola
   - sweets with artificial additives.

## What the child psychologist says

Dr Jemma Rosen-Webb:

'Kids will always challenge boundaries and make comparisons with what their friends are allowed to do or in this case eat. It's important to set boundaries that you are able to consistently stick to. There's nothing more reinforcing than being told you aren't allowed something, e.g. a bag of crisps, and learning that if you whine enough, you can sometimes have it after all.

Try redirecting your kids to healthier alternatives when you do not want them to eat junk, with only a brief explanation why.

For children who regularly spend time with grandparents or whose parents are separated, it is important to try to get some consistency (hard as this might be). If you are concerned that their eating of junk is out of control at those times, do try to talk to the other person about this.'

## What you can do about it

**If you don't want them to eat processed 'kiddy-marketed food', stop buying it!** Stand firm, stop buying those child-oriented cheeses and other special children's foods and just give them the normal stuff. OK, so they might still have it at friends' houses but that's better than at home too.

**But allow 'moderately naughty food' ... in moderation** Banning foods altogether can make them all the more alluring to kids. There may be some things that you absolutely don't want them to have but allowing goodies, junk food and the like occasionally and educating your children about their downsides are more likely to lead to a healthy approach overall.

*'We compromise by doing a "junk night" once a week – it helps a great deal. We have a night where everyone gets what they want to eat. So my son will*

*choose pizza, my daughter loves garlic bread ... that sort of thing. By doing this we give them a bit of what they fancy but also ensure that most of the time they get what they need.'*

Cassandra (son 9, daughter 7)

*'He's developed a really healthy attitude to chocolate. He knows and accepts he's allowed a tiny bit each day and on special occasions – it's not banned altogether, just moderated. But he also knows that whilst it tastes nice, it isn't that healthy and might damage his teeth.'*

Vicki (son 5)

**Speak out where needed** Talk to grandparents/other carers if they are making life difficult by stuffing the kids full of junk. Grandparents are renowned and indeed celebrated (by their grandchildren at least) for doling out the goodies. It's a shame to take away this element of the grandparent/grandchild relationship, so if it's a minor issue try to turn a blind eye as best you can. If it's causing problems back home or the children are with grandparents for significant periods, it could be time for a carefully worded chat.

---

**At what age ...?**

We asked at what age our parent panel's children could:

- Prepare a sandwich:
  - The average was age 6, with the range from 4 to 9.
- Prepare a simple breakfast such as cereal:
  - The average age was 5.4, with the range from 3 to 7.
- Be trusted to use sharp knives (with only a small chance of them losing a digit!):
  - Almost all said at age 9 or 10 – with supervision at first.

---

- Be able to cut up their own food:
  - Even the younger primary-school children could manage to cut up most foods – although nearly all our parents of 4–6-year-olds said cutting up meat/trickier stuff was something their child still needed help with.

## Further reading

- *Dealing with Difficult Eaters*, by Sally Child, published by Crimson

- *Manners from Heaven*, by Sean Davoren, published by Orion

- www.vegsoc.org (Vegetarian Society website, including information on healthy eating for vegetarian children, and recipes)

# 5
# Sleep

## Bedtime battles and morning mania

## The big issues

✔ Bedtimes

✔ Early mornings

✔ Night waking

Sleep problems are by no means the sole preserve of babies and toddlers. Yes, your days, or make that nights, of being woken three or four times will hopefully be over by now but some older children retain sleep issues or develop new ones such as bedwetting and sleepwalking. Things can get quite literally tiresome.

Most of us know all too well that a lack of sleep can make for a cranky kid (and as my family could testify about me, also a deeply cranky parent) but research also suggests getting sufficient zzzz's can make your child brainier and less prone to obesity. Studies show that a matter of just 30 minutes a day of lost sleep can impair a child's memory, vigilance and reaction times.

One perfectly serious study even made the ground-breaking assertion that a lack of sleep in children causes ... wait for it ... sleepiness. Who'd have thought it?

## Bedtimes

Children can arm themselves with an imaginative arsenal of ways to delay crossing the border into the land of nod. There's the Jack-in-the-box type (get them into bed and they spring out again), the bookworm who sneakily reads by torchlight and the ones who invent 1,001 really quite credible reasons why you must go back to their room. All you probably want to do is ensure they get a decent night's sleep and a bit of the evening to yourself, so what's the best way of going about it?

## Background info

- According to a German study quoted in the journal *Sleep*, 20–40 per cent of 9-year-olds in the study had trouble getting to sleep.

- Our parent panel's typical bedtimes are:
  - 4–7-year-olds: between 7 and 8pm
  - 8–11-year-olds: between 8 and 9pm

- Among our parents, 65 per cent relax bedtimes at weekends and during school holidays, and a further 13 per cent during the holidays but not at weekends during term time.

- By age 7 or 8, most children are reading their own bedtime story. Typical approaches include:

*'I stopped reading to him when he was 8 (sadly) – it was his preference but he often sidles in to hear my daughter's stories if they are old favourites. He reads to himself now.'*

Katherine (son 8, daughter 4)

*'We occasionally read to them as a treat, but don't do it every night any more. We stopped this when they were both confident readers.'*

Mandy (daughters 9 and 6)

*'Occasionally I'll read a story at bedtime, but they tend to read themselves now. Lights out is at 8.45,*

*before that they can read, draw, listen to an audio tape, etc.'*

Lynsey (sons 10 and 7)

- Many parents on our panel let their child read to themselves once in bed. Some have a set time when reading has to stop and lights go out, others don't.

*'They can read, but they can't get out of bed or mess around. Once they're in bed, that's it!'*

Coral (sons 7 and 5)

## What the sleep expert says

Dr Pat Spungin, child psychologist and author of *Silent Nights*:

'Even for school-age children, bedtime routines – bath, teeth, story (or for older children them reading in bed) – remain important and beneficial – they can make a significant difference to how easily a child settles at bedtime.

Allowing 10 or 15 minutes of winding-down time, with the light on for reading or listening to recorded stories or music, until they're more relaxed and ready to sleep, can also help. Watching television or using games consoles at bedtime is best avoided, as these can be too stimulating.

One potential reason for children resisting going to bed is because their bedtime is too early. It's worth starting with the time they have to be up for school or wake up naturally, then subtracting the amount of sleep a child that age typically needs [see next page].

Another cause of school-age children being reluctant to go to bed is anxiety   perhaps worries over bullying or tension at home. Asking gently whether there is anything on their mind might get to the bottom of this.'

## What you can do about it

**Get the bedtime right** Generally, most primary-school kids need 10–11 hours sleep, although for some 10- and 11-year-olds this will be nearer 9 or 10. Work back from the time they need to be up for school (on weekdays) or their normal waking-up time if earlier, and use that as a starting point. Remember, though, that children do vary with their sleep needs and there is no 'one-size-fits-all' bedtime or amount of sleep for a particular age. Some will be exhausted even on 11 hours a night, others barely yawning with considerably less.

**Follow a set routine on school nights at least, if possible** Routines aren't every family's cuppa but they can make a significant difference to how much your child pushes back at bedtime. If they know they always have to go upstairs at, say, 7.15 on a school night, have a bath, do teeth, etc. and get into bed by 8, they are generally less likely to start complaining.

**Allow some deviation at the weekends and in holidays** Most school-age children can understand that school nights mean an earlier 'set' bedtime but that you relax the rules a bit, perhaps on Saturday nights, or during holidays.

*'During the week they have to go to sleep at bedtime. At weekends or during holidays they might be allowed to chat (they share a room) for half an hour before sleeping. This is conditional – if they carry on when they're meant to be sleeping, they won't be allowed to next time.'*

Mandy (daughters 9 and 6)

**Keep the pre-bedtime period relaxing** Avoid TV and computer games close to bedtime. Watching TV/DVDs in the early evening has been associated with sleep problems and could leave your child over-stimulated and unable to drop off. Steer clear of caffeinated drinks and lots of chocolate too. Exercise generally helps people sleep better, but not if it's within the last couple of hours before bed.

Limit running around and rough and tumble and steer them towards quieter activities, such as a book or story CD. A nice bath should help too. If you still read them bedtime stories, choose something fairly gentle rather than overly exciting and perhaps keep your voice calm and low towards the end.

**Try to help them to relax after lights out** Some children's minds are especially active, making it harder for them to 'switch off'. Relaxation tapes, gentle music, and even meditation techniques are worth a try (try getting them to imagine their body sinking into the bed/warm sand on the beach, starting with their toes and slowly working through every bit until their head).

*'I suggest things for him to think about if he seems a bit too active to sleep. Sometimes it's making up a story about a favourite subject in his head, or thinking of the*

*nicest things he did that day, or trying to remember the names of all the children in his class of 30!'*

Vicki (son 5)

**Take away as many excuses as you can for delaying tactics** Anticipate all those little demands for you to return to their room or excuses for them to get out of bed. Ensure they have a drink of water to hand, have been to the loo just before bed, the light is at the right level if they have a nightlight, etc. It's worth actually asking at lights out 'Have you got everything you need?' to pre-empt anything else.

**Keep firm and consistent bedtime rules** Firmly but calmly insist they go back to bed/stop calling out. If needed, warn them at bedtime that you'll ignore any further comments (emergencies like being sick excluded) and are busy now (with something that sounds boring to them so they don't feel they're missing out).

If you do need to interact after bedtime, be as dull as possible – no chatting. Consistency is key – if eventually you give in, it suggests that if they keep calling out for long enough you will come back up so they might try it on in the same way in future.

*'Once he is in bed he has to stay there – unless he needs the toilet.'*

Jo (son 5)

*'We had a phase of her getting out of bed and coming back downstairs. We ignored her if she did this and turned off the TV until she went back up. It was annoying but it did sort it out quickly.'*

Karen (daughters 7, 6 and 4)

**Explain why sleep is important!** Sometimes, amid shouting and pleading with offspring, it's easy to forget that it might be worth actually explaining why they need to do something. A gentle reminder that they'll be too tired to enjoy X, where X is an appealing activity the next day, can work well.

**But do consider if there's something worrying/scaring them at bedtime** If they're scared of the dark, get a night-light. If they're worried about monsters or similar, try making up a rhyme together about banishing the monsters but do also tell them firmly that there aren't any.

**And if all else fails** For those Jack-in-the-box types, you have three main options:

1 Keep returning them to bed, minimising interaction with them until they give up (this could take a while and a lot of patience – best avoided if you might lose your temper).

2 Keep them in their room. Close the door. If they can open it themselves (the case for most of this age group), consider holding it shut – but stay quietly just outside to ensure they're OK.

3 Use a reward system (see page 2) to encourage behaviour change.

## Early mornings

*'J wakes up at 6.30am no matter whether it's a school day, holiday or weekend. I thought he'd have grown out*

*of it by now. I'm a single parent so it's relentless – I can barely function at that time and long for a lie in until ... 7.30!'*

If your alarm clock sits redundant because your offspring have taken on its job all too capably (but unfortunately without a function to actually choose your wake-up time), it might be scant consolation that those teenage mammoth lie-ins are not so many years off now and it'll be time for you to get revenge by waking them up before noon when they don't like it.

Some children are natural 'larks' (if yours is and you aren't, you have my commiserations) but, with others, early waking could be a habit or caused by something 'external'. The good news is, with the latter two explanations, there is hope of getting them to stay eyes shut under that duvet for longer.

## Background info

Our parent panel have different approaches to dealing with early morning waking but the vast majority are resigned to it and many let their school-age children amuse themselves in their room or quietly downstairs until a slightly more earthly hour.

> 'K at 7 can get up, go downstairs and get herself some cereal and drink.'
>
> Sue (daughter, 7)

## What the sleep expert says

Dr Pat Spungin:

'Children waking early can be draining for you and them. It's often said that people are born larks or owls, but research suggests only 10–15 per cent of children have a firm genetic predisposition towards waking up early.

For the remaining 85–90 per cent, one of the most common reasons for early waking is simply that they have had enough sleep. If your child wakes up lively after a full night's sleep and doesn't seem unduly tired, they don't have a sleep problem – rather they might just have developed a habit of waking up early, whatever the original reason. As with all habits, this can be hard to break at first but it is possible to reset their body clock, given time and perseverance.

Try gradually moving bedtime later so that they're going to bed later and hopefully waking up later – although this doesn't always work and some children will continue to wake early regardless of their bedtime.

Another cause of waking early is your child's sleep environment. It's worth going into their bedroom early in the morning, to see if the room is too bright, or noises could be waking them up. It could be that the central heating rattles or there's heavy traffic outside, neighbours are up and about and can be heard from their bedroom, or the like. Alternatively, they might be too warm or cold, hungry or needing the toilet.'

## What you can do about it

**Try a later bedtime** If you tend to put your child to bed early as they're exhausted by 6.30 or 7, it's worth experimenting and putting up with a few days of grouchiness in the late afternoons/evenings, to see if this makes a difference in the mornings. You might need to adjust things gradually over, say, a week, going 15 minutes later a day.

If they weren't always early risers, it's especially worth trying this, given children need less sleep as they get older. This won't work for everyone – as mentioned above, some kids just seem programmed to get up at a particular time, in which case your only option is to get an early night or start encouraging them to entertain themselves quietly!

*'He would still wake at the same time even if we put him to bed later, so we stick with the same routine to ensure he gets the 12 hours he needs. We go to bed earlier and as long as we get our eight hours we're fine with it now.'*

Karen (son, 6)

**Check for external triggers** Does it get too light in their room (invest in some black-out blinds) or is there traffic noise or perhaps they're woken by a younger sibling in the next room? Try some white noise – a desk fan works a treat for this in my son's room and prevents him being woken up by noise from outside his window.

**Provide younger ones, who can't yet tell the time, with a 'getting-up signal'** You can buy special simplified alarm clocks for younger children or put a bedside light on a timer switch. Until the clock/light signals it's OK to get up, they have to stay in bed. Well, that's the idea. Some will resolutely ignore the fact the clock bunny's eyes aren't open yet/the light isn't on, but it's worth a try, especially combined with tons of praise or a reward chart incentive.

**And if all else fails** If your child is just a natural early waker, encourage them to amuse themselves for a while, either in their room or, if you feel they can be trusted without adult supervision, downstairs.

> *'She can get up and do what she likes. I am usually half awake and can hear her in the background. She watches TV or a movie but doesn't do her own breakfast yet.'*
>
> Angela (daughter, 7)

> *'They can watch TV quietly. On weekends and holidays we leave out a carton of juice and a cereal bar, then they have their proper breakfast when I get up.'*
>
> Bev (sons 8 and 5)

# Night waking

It's not at all unusual for school-age children to have interrupted sleep and there are lots of reasons for this – some longstanding and others new. Bedwetting, fear of the dark and nightmares are all common triggers for that shout of 'Mum/Dad' in the wee (pardon the pun if you're parent to a bedwetter) small hours.

## Background info

- Depending on which research you look at, 10–15 per cent of children sleepwalk at least occasionally.

- Studies suggest around 30 per cent of 4-year-olds, 10 per cent of 6-year-olds and 4 per cent of 10-year-olds wet the bed.

## What the sleep expert says

Dr Pat Spungin:

'Most children have nightmares at least occasionally but for some they're a more common occurrence. They occur during REM sleep, typically during the later part of the night. Children might wake up scared and remember these dreams, possibly referring to them later on. Nightmares are usually associated with anxiety and stress and can be caused by scary stories, violence on TV, in films or computer games.

Night terrors are sometimes confused with nightmares but are quite different, occurring within the first few hours after falling asleep. They can be very frightening to parents but the child is unaware of what is happening and a child having a night terror will be very difficult to rouse or comfort and could get more upset if you try, whereas those having nightmares can normally be woken up and consoled relatively easily.

Children in the middle of a night terror may suddenly appear to wake up screaming, scared, confused, incoherent and hallucinating. Their pupils will be dilated, they might sweat and have a fast heart rate. A terror might last for 10 to 30 minutes but will not be remembered the following day. The cause is unknown although they might be associated with overtiredness. They tend to occur most between the ages of 3 and 8 and often run in families.

Sleepwalking, meanwhile, is more common among boys than girls and usually occurs between ages 3 and 7, stopping by around 13. Patterns vary, with some only sleepwalking occasionally, and others doing it every night. Sleepwalking episodes normally take place in the first part of a night, a couple of hours after falling asleep and last from 5 to 20 minutes. The child may get out of bed and walk around, in or out of the room. They might talk or attempt to, and might urinate, unfortunately not necessarily in the toilet. A sleepwalking child will usually not answer if you try and talk to them.

Bedwetting is a fairly common problem in the first years of primary school and can be a source of great embarrassment for children, not to mention an inconvenience for parents who will be woken in the night and have to change bedding. It's normally a concern if it continues beyond the age of around 6. It can have psychological or physical triggers and, if it's a persistent problem, it's certainly worth seeking advice from your doctor, who will be able to refer you for specialist support to tackle the problem if needed.'

## What you can do about it

**Take night-time fears seriously** If a child is having nightmares or is afraid, this is not the time for ignoring them, telling them not to be silly (a fear or bad dream might feel very real to them) or being visibly annoyed that they've woken you up.

**Give reassurance** Often a hug and a brief chat along the lines of 'It's OK, it was a dream and wasn't real' is enough.

As soon as their fears are calmed, call it a night, though, or you risk creating an unnecessary habit of a cosy middle-of-the-night chat.

*'If she has a nightmare she is allowed to come into bed with us until she feels ready to go back to her own – this usually takes 15 minutes or so. Usually she just wants to debrief from the nightmare – to tell us about it, and we chat about how great it is that these things aren't real, and what an amazing imagination she must have.'*

Lynsey (daughters 9 and 6)

**Tell, and if needed and possible, show them that what they're scared of isn't real** So if they think there's a bogeyman in the wardrobe, open it so they can see there isn't (within reason – you'll be able to tell if this is getting out of hand when you're spending hours checking every cupboard in the house in rotation!).

**Come up with a strategy together** Make it very clear you *know* there are no witches in the wardrobe, but if they still want to, they can have a rhyme or statement to say if they're scared. A short bedtime check or a note beside the bed/on the door saying 'No entry to monsters' is fine too, if it makes them feel better.

*'I instruct one of his cuddlies to stay awake and keep an eye on him and he's fine with that!'*

Bev (sons 8 and 5)

*'We got him to write a little notice for the door saying 'No monsters allowed' and also had a made-up rhyme*

to say at bedtime to ward them off. I did keep saying
that I was sure there were no monsters too.'

Karen (son 6)

**Distract them by suggesting something lovely to think
about at bedtime** It could be remembering a recent
holiday or a gentle story, or thinking of cuddling you –
anything that will bring pleasant associations to stop them
worrying about their fear.

**Think about what might be triggering the nightmares**
Bad dreams can be associated with stress, inappropriate
TV imagery, scary bedtime stories, or a recent upsetting
experience (bullying, parents breaking up or arguing a lot,
bereavement). Talking through their fears/anxieties in the
day might help.

'We try and limit scary stuff on TV and in books. He
doesn't watch anything more potent than CBeebies most
of the time but baddies in some of the kids' films we
have on DVD can trigger a nightmare. As can the scene
in The Wizard of Oz where the wicked witch melts.
Turns out that was much scarier than I remembered it
being as a child, and we found that out the hard way!'

Judy (son 5)

**Note that some nightmares have no apparent reason**
Just because your child is having them doesn't mean
something terrible has happened in the day.

**Don't wake sleepwalkers** Waking a sleepwalker is quite
difficult and can really upset them.

**... or those having night terrors** Even though they can be scary for you, keep as calm as you can, and gently reassure your child.

*'For quite a long time we didn't know what they were and we weren't responding properly. Then we followed advice to just comfort her and calm her down through reassurance but not really talk to her. Through suggestion I can calm her much more quickly, because she can sort of hear us, she just can't respond. So I might say "It's OK, everything is fine, Mum's magic kiss is going to send you back to sleep now" and kiss her on the forehead. That sort of thing seems to work well and she will go back to sleep as if nothing happened.'*

Siobhan (daughter 5)

**Guide or carry sleepwalkers back to bed** Make the environment as safe as possible in case it happens again, e.g. put a chain on or double-lock your front door.

**Try waking them first** If it happens at a similar time each night, try waking them just before for a moment. This can break the pattern if you do it for a few days.

**Don't make it a big issue** Provide reassurance when they wake up if needed but don't make a big issue of it. In the morning, it's unlikely they'll remember but if they become upset or worried about sleepwalking, reassure them that it is normal, nothing to worry about and they will grow out of it. If they have no recollection of it, it won't help to discuss things and might just add to anxiety.

*'It's upsetting to see your child apparently so frightened,
but actually they never remember anything in the
morning, so my advice is just to keep calm and relaxed,
lay them down and stroke them and see it through
until they go back to sleep. Don't ask what's wrong or
anything like that, which makes it worse, and try not to
get angry or frustrated, just stay calm and reassuring.'*

Siobhan (daughter 5)

### Don't embarrass, punish or blame your child for bedwetting

It is *extremely* unlikely they are doing it on purpose (see
above). They will probably find what's happened embarrassing and upsetting, so be sensitive to this (for example,
if they're going on a sleepover, only mention it to the other
parent when your child is out of earshot).

### Consider external triggers as stress can cause bedwetting

This could be goings-on at school, bereavement, divorce or
illness.

*'L had a phase of wetting the bed about six months ago,
which coincided with the arrival of the new baby.'*

Lynsey (boys 10 and 7)

*'My 11-year-old sometimes wets the bed (although
he hasn't done it for about four months now). It was
usually if he was overtired or something different was
happening at school.'*

Anon (sons 11 and 7, daughter 9)

### Limit drinks before bedtime

But do encourage consumption
earlier in the day. If they're not drinking much at school
and then gulping down litres just before bedtime, this

could be contributing. Also avoid diuretic drinks such as those with caffeine.

*'I am careful to try to give the majority of drinks earlier in the evening. I would never refuse a drink request but limit it to water only.'*
Anon (sons 11 and 7, daughter 9)

*'We were referred to the enuresis clinic and the first thing the doc asked was about how much he drank during the day. It turned out it wasn't nearly enough and this was the first thing that had to be addressed – otherwise he wouldn't drink much all day and then drank too much at night.'*
Catherine (son 7, daughter 5)

**Encourage two wees, not just one, before bed!** For some children, bedwetting can be limited if they do one toilet trip, say before their shower/bath, and then another immediately before bedtime, around 5 or 10 minutes after the first.

**Kit yourself out** Waterproof sheets can go under or over the normal sheets and modern versions don't have to be the plasticky, crinkly, sweaty horrors many of us endured as kids. Keep spare bedding etc. close to hand for quick changes at night.

**Try 'lifting'** This means whisking your child out of bed late in the evening – usually at your own bedtime, for a pre-emptive wee. Do it with minimal disturbance and they'll be straight back to sleep – if they wake up at all.

'We make sure they go to the toilet at bedtime and we "wee" them when we go to bed between 10 and 11pm.'

Coralie (boys 7 and 5)

**Consider an enuresis alarm for regular wetters** This is a small clip that attaches to their pants/PJs and goes off when they wee.

'My daughter wet the bed until last year. We had an alarm that really helped and more or less solved the problem over a three-month period.'

Amanda (daughter 10, son 8)

'T still wore pull-ups at night until he was 6 and a half. Every morning they were wet and now and again we would try to get him to go without but he always wet the bed. We sorted it out with an enuresis alarm – it was brilliant. Within 10 days he was dry and almost never wets the bed now.'

Catherine (son 7, daughter 5)

**Get more help** If any sleep problem is causing your child to be exhausted or upset on a regular basis and/or it's interfering with everyday life, seek help via your GP or directly from a sleep clinic.

## Further reading

- *Silent Nights,* by Dr Pat Spungin, published by Prentice Hall
- www.eric.org.uk (bedwetting information and support)

# 6
# Growing up fast

## From them venturing out alone to bl**dy swearing

# The big issues

- ✔ Out on their own
- ✔ In on their own
- ✔ You're not wearing *that*!
- ✔ Bl\*\*dy swearing

One minute they're babes in arms, the next they're trying to end up in the arms of a boyfriend/girlfriend, or attempting to persuade you of the appropriateness of that alarmingly short skirt, or going to the park with their mates, or using far too colourful language.

Of course we need to foster independence in our children, letting them make their own choices and equipping them with the skills to deal with this sometimes big, bad world we inhabit; but, for many of us, it all feels too much too soon.

Media, merchandise and marketing don't help those wanting to try and keep their children, well, children a little longer, with a barrage of imagery which seemingly encourages kids to be mini adults when they're only a few years out of nappies.

Pester power and peer pressure play a part too – your child comes home from school declaring 'But all my friends are allowed to …' which may or may not be true. With all these issues, it's certainly a good idea to check if they're trying it on/the other children are exaggerating somewhat.

# Out on their own

*'She says all her friends are allowed out together but I
don't feel comfortable with this yet. They're only 10. Am
I being overprotective?'*

Whilst many of our generation were allowed to venture
out at a relatively young age, most of today's primary
schoolers have much less freedom. How often do you see
8-year-olds walking to school without an accompanying
adult these days? Some schools don't even allow children
below year 5 or 6 to leave without a grown-up.

Clearly, unless you plan on gluing your child to your
side well into adulthood, at some stage you've got to let
them go out alone (or at least without adult supervision).
How else will they learn to be streetwise, to assess risks
and to feel confident when you're no longer whisking them
around in the car or walking beside them?

There's no universal answer as to when the right age is
and, surprisingly perhaps, there's no law on the matter.
What's appropriate for you and your child will be different
from what's appropriate for their classmates, cousins or
friends. That said, it is unlikely an under-9-year-old will
have the wherewithal to walk/cycle to school alone (and
many children of this age and under struggle to judge the
speed of cars on the roads). With slightly older children,
it's a case of using your own judgement about when, where
and how, and standing by your decision even when your
child whines that 'It's so unfair … everybody else … '.

## Background info

- According to the Walk to School Campaign, in 1971 80 per cent of 7–8-year-olds travelled to school without an adult but by 2006 (the latest year for which figures were available at the time of writing) the figure had dropped to 12 per cent of 7–10-year-olds. At the age of 11, almost every child used to walk to school alone; now this is down to 55 per cent and falling.

- In our parent panel survey, of the children aged 9–11:
    - 49 per cent are allowed to go to the local park without a grown-up (usually with friends)
    - 37 per cent are allowed to go to the local 'corner' shop without a grown-up
    - 45 per cent are allowed to walk or cycle to school without a grown-up.

## What the child psychologist says

Dr Jemma Rosen-Webb:

'The journey towards independence begins early on. Children who feel secure that their parent will protect and care about them begin to make their first steps into exploring the wider world. Independence continues to develop with separations for nursery, then school, then overnight stays at friends' houses, etc.

Just as toddlers need to know they have a safe place (their parent) to explore the world from, children nearing their teenage years need their parents both to protect them but also promote their independence. Being allowed more independence in a gradual way promotes confidence and self-belief.

How much independence is allowed is a very individual decision and should be based on your child's age, ability, where they want to go, with whom and for how long. You will also probably base your decision on what you were allowed to do as a child and how appropriate you felt that was.'

## What you can do about it

**Work out what's appropriate for *your* child, in your area** Maybe others in the class *are* starting to walk to school alone or go to the park without an adult (although do check this is true as children are great at exaggerating – one kid is allowed to and suddenly they're claiming everyone is), but if, for whatever reason, you think your child isn't ready, stand by your conviction. There can be vast differences in individual children's maturity, how much they've experienced independence so far and what families are comfortable with, not to mention the nature of where you live.

> 'Unfortunately we live in an isolated rural area so it's impossible for them to go anywhere alone. If we lived in a village or town I'd allow my 10-year-old to go to the shop or park now.'
>
> Vanessa (sons 10 and 8)

> 'I am starting to let her have more independence now but it's quite difficult and she isn't the most mature for her age. We often argue about it – she thinks she should

*be allowed to do more than I let her. I'd rather wrap her up in cotton wool and keep her at home or with me still!'*

Alex (daughters 11 and 7, son 4)

**Start off slowly and build up** Begin with small trips, perhaps delivering letters to the post box or dropping your child part of the way to school and walking the rest. See how it goes and take things from there. Make each trip slightly further as their and your confidence grows. Some parents do go along a little behind their child the first time or two, either in the car or on foot, and either telling them or not.

*'I let my 8-year-old go into the shop on her own and I wait outside.'*

Lisa (daughters 8 and 6)

*'We stuck with short distances only at first – school is a 10-minute walk and I followed behind at some distance with my younger child.'*

Marieke (son 10, daughter 7)

**Allow walking home from school before walking to school initially** The thinking here is that you wouldn't know for a while if they didn't arrive at school but would know more quickly if they didn't make it home (assuming you or another carer is in).

*'I allowed them to walk home from school first, so that way I would know if they were late.'*

Mandy (daughters 17 and 11, sons 15 and 5)

**Remember there's safety in numbers (usually)** If your child can walk to school with the neighbour's kids or go somewhere with friends, this might be better than alone, as long as they won't distract each other when crossing roads or encourage each other into mischief.

> 'The summer he finished primary school, he was allowed to go to the park – so aged 11 – and in the company of at least one other sensible friend.'
>
> Josie (son 13, daughters 11 and 7)

> 'I have just started letting my 10-year-old go to the park and shops but only if she is with a friend and has her mobile with her.'
>
> Helen (daughter 10, son 8)

**Enforce a 3Ws rule** Before they leave, insist they tell you:

- who they're going with
- where they're going
- when they'll be back.

**Remind them about safety issues** Before their first trip out alone (and subsequently if you think the message might have been forgotten), think about whether you need to go through road safety and 'stranger danger' advice again.

**Ensure they know where you'll be and how to contact you in an emergency** Write down your mobile number/enter it into their phone – in the heat of the moment, they might forget it.

**Suggest who to ask if they need help** A police officer/ member of the emergency services if they can see one, shop assistant or someone with children (I try not to stereo-type with my son but for convenience tell him to look for a mum with kids) is probably a better bet than just going for whoever is nearest, urgent emergencies excepted.

**Make use of mobile phones** Even if you'd still rather they didn't have their own, perhaps you could have a spare Pay as You Go 'family' phone they can take when going somewhere without an adult. Remind them to be discreet with its use, especially in less salubrious areas.

> 'One rule is they have to take their phone, turn it on and answer it.'
>
> Amanda (daughter 11, son 9)

> 'She has to be back at an exact time in order to be allowed to do it again. She must also take her phone and answer whenever I call.'
>
> Amanda (daughters 11 and 8)

**Try to keep your cool!** If you're the worrying type (count me in for that), this is easier said than done, but remember they are statistically more likely to be struck by lightning than abducted by a stranger (so perhaps don't let them out in a thunderstorm?).

---

**Stranger danger advice**

The charity Kidscape's guidelines on safety recommend that children need to know how:

- TO BE SAFE. Tell children that everyone has rights, and that no one should take away their right to be safe.
- TO PROTECT THEIR BODIES. Their bodies belong to them, particularly the private parts covered by their swimsuits.
- TO SAY NO. It's all right to say no to anyone, if that person is trying to harm them.
- TO TELL. Assure children that no matter what happens, you will not be angry with them – and that you want them to tell you about any incident.
- TO BE BELIEVED. If they go to an adult for help, they need to know that they will be believed and supported.
- NOT TO KEEP SECRETS. Teach children that some kinds of secrets should never be kept: child molesters will often say that a touch or kiss is 'our secret'.
- TO REFUSE TOUCHES. They should not be forced to hug or kiss anyone if they do not want to.
- NOT TO TALK TO STRANGERS. As most well-meaning adults or teenagers do not approach children who are alone, unless they are lost or in distress, teach children to ignore any such approach: they should pretend not to hear and quickly walk or run away.
- TO BREAK RULES. Sometimes it is all right to break rules in order to protect themselves and stay safe: to run away, for example, or to yell and make a fuss – even to lie and kick to get away from danger.

Guidelines reproduced with permission from Kidscape, www.kidscape.org.uk

# In on their own

*'My gut feel is she will be fine if I go out for an hour or two but I'm not 100 per cent sure and it plays on my mind.'*

Again, as with going out alone, there's no law regarding the age children can be left at home unsupervised. However, it is an offence to leave a child home alone if it places them at risk, and until they reach 16 your children are your legal responsibility.

Many 10- and 11-year-olds will be OK for a short period but most people agree it's unwise to leave them for more than an hour or two and not all day or overnight.

Again, this comes down to your child's level of maturity and independence – some 11-year-olds won't bat an eyelid about being left at home, others will hate the idea, yet more still will create hurricane-force havoc in the house if left unsupervised for more than about 30 seconds.

## Background info

- The law: as above, there is no legal age at which you are allowed to leave a child home alone. However, you could be prosecuted for neglect (and face a lot of contact with social services) if you leave a child unsupervised 'in a manner likely to cause them unnecessary suffering or injury to health'.

- The NSPCC recommends under 12s are only left for 'very short periods' (this isn't defined) and that under 16s should not be left alone overnight.

- Among the parent panel, 42 per cent of over-9-year-olds are left at home alone for short spells, although this was more prevalent among 10- and 11-year-olds.

## What the child psychologist says

Dr Jemma Rosen-Webb:

'Again, it comes down to your child's age, maturity and how comfortable you and they are with the idea of staying in at home alone. Start with short time periods and make sure they are clear what to do if any problems arise. It's important to let them know that you trust them and that it is very unlikely that anything will go wrong but that you want to make sure they know what to do if needed.'

## What you can do about it

**Stick with short periods at this age** As with going out alone, start off small and build up – keep it to things like you taking a 10-minute trip to the shop while they stay behind.

> 'I feel pretty happy leaving him for 10 or 15 minutes while I go to the corner shop but probably wouldn't do more than that for a while yet.'
>
> Catherine (son 10)

**Ensure they know what to do in an emergency** Leave your mobile phone number clearly out and tell them where it is, where you're going and when you'll be back. Remind them about dialling 999 in a real emergency. Discuss fire safety and escape routes (obviously trying not to freak them out in the process! 'It's very, very unlikely but you need to know just in case ...').

> 'I gave them the home phone, dialled my mobile and told them they just had to hit redial to call me.'
>
> Jo (sons 15, 11 and 3, daughter 9)

**Have clear rules** Our parent panel's main rules included not using the oven/cooker/kettle, and not opening the front door to anyone.

> *'I let my eldest stay alone for half an hour now. Our rules are no answering the door and no making toast.'*
> Vanessa (sons 10 and 8)

> *'Front door locked, don't answer the door. Answer the phone (in case it's me) and say that Mum is in the shower. No oven, knives, or "fixing the fire".'*
> Amanda (daughters 11 and 8)

> *'I made sure my son's mobile was on and fully charged, told him not to answer the door to strangers but said he could answer the phone and agreed some simple rules with him for if there was an emergency.'*
> Josie (son 13, daughters 11 and 7)

**Initially, consider asking a trusted neighbour to be on call** It'll be reassuring for both you and your child if there's someone nearby in case of an emergency.

> *'The first few times I rang a neighbour to make sure she was about.'*
> Josie (son 13, daughters 11 and 7)

**Never expect primary schoolers to care for younger siblings alone** It's one thing for a 10- or 11-year-old to be home alone for an hour, but quite another to babysit a younger sister or brother. Whilst there's no law on babysitting ages, the NSPCC recommends a minimum of 16.

# You're not wearing *that*!

*'I cannot believe what some of the girls in my daughter's class are wearing to parties. At 9, several of them are in heels and make-up. I don't want her in white ankle socks and am realistic, but I don't want this either – it's too much too soon.'*

There's long been a clash between what children (especially girls) want to wear and what their parents prefer: my mum and aunt battled to be allowed to wear denim in the 1960s – grandma thought it 'unladylike'. But it seems, with increasing media influences and a blurring of the lines between adult and children's clothing, this sartorial clash of generations has intensified recently.

High street shops don't quite brim with the provocative girls' clothing that has been lambasted in the newspapers recently (push-up bras for 9-year-olds, etc.) but there is a widespread pressure for young girls, in particular, to dress, and act, grown-up – too soon for most parents' likings.

Wearing make-up is another issue to contend with – firmly banned in the vast majority of primary schools but less clear-cut outside the school gates.

## Background info

- Almost all our parent panel let their children have input into their choice of clothes but take final decisions on what's bought themselves. The only exceptions are a few whose children don't care what they wear, so the parents choose alone.

- Most of our parent panel allowed girls to wear a bit of lip gloss/nail varnish from around age 6. Other make-up was still not allowed by the vast majority by the end of primary school.

## What the child psychologist says

Dr Jemma Rosen-Webb:

> 'Parents need to be mindful of children being exposed to things that they are not emotionally and developmentally ready for in many areas of life, from watching scary or violent films to alcohol (and drugs) and sexual imagery. It is important to think about the messages that your child is receiving from the world around them. Girls especially are taught through magazines, pop videos and TV shows that looking and dressing in particular (and often sexual) ways are the only ways to feel good about themselves.

> It is important that children get a positive sense of self not only from how they look (and dress) but also from their own abilities and qualities. Helping your child to feel good about these things may reduce the passion with which they argue about the clothing they "have to have". Even if it does not reduce disagreements about clothing and make-up in the short term, in the long run it will help them learn to value themselves as a person and not just for their appearance.'

## What you can do about it

**Remember that you are the decision maker** No matter how strong that pester power gets, with children this age the final decision over what is worn remains *yours*. Who cares if every other 9-year-old in the land wears sequinned crop tops or scarily short skirts? If you aren't comfortable with it, stand firm.

**But present and discuss your reasons** It's worth calmly explaining your reasons over the cacophony of their complaints that they hate you/it's *so* not fair, etc. It might make no difference, of course, but it's worth a try.

> *'I try to stand firm to the pester power. If I give the impression I'm going to give in or I'm saying no for the sake of it, she sees through it. I usually do give a reason – it's too grown up, etc.- and occasionally it seems to sink in with her.'*
>
> Victoria (daughter, 9)

**Compromise sometimes and pick your battles** Like it or not, children do grow up a bit more quickly these days and wearing pretty smock dresses just doesn't cut it for most girls over the age of 5. Your daughter probably just wants to fit in with her peers.

You might stick to your guns about refusing the miniscule mini-skirt and full make-up, but could perhaps allow some clear lip gloss, some glitter, or subtle nail varnish for a special occasion. It's also important to let them wear an outfit of their choosing sometimes, if you merely think it looks ridiculous rather than being inappropriate. As children grow up, it's healthy for them to develop their own sense of style.

> *'I lay down the law where I think it's non-negotiable but I'm happy to compromise where I don't feel it's so important. So, for example, my youngest can't have*

*her ears pierced, but last week she went to church
in a leotard and cycling shorts – I felt it wasn't that
important.'*

Josie (son 13, daughters 11 and 7)

*'I still do the clothes shopping, so I veto anything
inappropriate. My daughter does get a choice, though,
and has definite likes and dislikes, which I listen to.
Some of her skirts are shorter than we would prefer, but
I agree to them with leggings as a compromise.'*

Claire (daughter 7)

*'The peer pressure to wear nail polish and lip gloss
starts quite young. We don't want our child to be
"different" and so have allowed her to wear a little
when she goes to a party.'*

Allison (daughter 7, son 4)

**Let them experiment and dress up at home** Girls have
played with make-up and clip-clopped around in their
mothers' high heels for as long as high heels have existed.
It's harmless, healthy fun and can sometimes make make-up
seem less illicit, cutting down the requests to wear it out.

*'My youngest daughter sometimes likes her nails painted
and a bit of lip gloss. She's probably been doing it for
the last couple of years but I feel it's harmless. I can
remember putting on my mum's make-up and perfume
when I was a little girl and strutting around in her heels
and loving it!'*

Josie (son 13, daughters 11 and 7)

**First bras**

It's not uncommon for girls to reach puberty in the primary-school years and so bras can be an issue even for under-11s. It's something of a rite of passage to get your first bra but can also be fraught – some girls are embarrassed that they need one before their classmates, others distraught that they don't when everyone else does.

Early developers as well as late can face teasing, especially when changing for PE/swimming. Be sensitive to the fact that even if your daughter doesn't physically need a bra yet, she might want one to fit in. If so, an appropriate 'bra-like' crop top might help. These are also good for that in-between stage when a bra isn't yet needed but girls can feel exposed under school shirts and don't want to wear a bog-standard vest.

When it comes to buying her first proper bra, if your daughter seems awkward discussing the subject with you, perhaps rope a trusted (by both of you) aunt or female family friend in to help.

Go to a proper lingerie department or store to get her measured (many daughters will find this excruciatingly embarrassing – your best bet is to at least explain that it can be harmful to wear the wrong size). Be sensitive about it all; announcing that your daughter needs a bra (or has started her periods) to the entire family can be pretty mortifying for a pre-teen girl.

*'My older daughter started wearing bras in the summer – she hates it and feels different from most of her friends who don't need one yet. We had a very nice lady in the shop who was as discreet as possible but L found it mortifying and only liked it when we went for coffee and cake afterwards. I made a point of getting rid of the other two children so we could go alone and I have since bought her matching sets of underwear to try and make it fun and lovely, but she's not ready for it and at 11 finds it tough.'*

Josie (son 13, daughters 11 and 7)

> *'A few months before you think she'll need a bra, get her used to wearing crop tops to make it less of a scary transition.'*
>
> Amanda (daughters 11 and 8)

## More girl talk: periods

Starting to menstruate as young as age 9 is not unheard of and research shows that 12 per cent of girls do so before the end of primary school. If you sense your daughter might begin to menstruate soon, she might be embarrassed to talk about it or ask for advice. Periods usually start around a year after a height and weight growth spurt, a year after breasts begin to develop and after a girl has reached seven stone in weight.

If you haven't already had a chat about puberty (see page 160) and think it's around the corner, it's a wise move to broach the subject now. Provide her with some sanitary towels in case it happens and she doesn't want to tell you straight away. Suggest she keeps a couple with her at school just in case, or knows who to go to if she starts when there, e.g. the school nurse.

If you can find a way to talk about this sort of thing now, you'll increase the chances of her being happier talking to you about sex and contraception when the time comes.

## Ear piercing

Daughters (and some sons) nagging about wanting pierced ears is a really common issue with this age group. A key question to ask yourself, and your child, is whether they're responsible and mature enough to look after their ears afterwards to prevent infection.

> *'My 6-year-old wants earrings and I have said no, not until she is in secondary school. I had mine done when I*

> was 9, I didn't look after them properly and they became infected.'
>
> Jo (daughter 6, son 2)

Remember also that some primary schools don't allow earrings at school, which means they will have to have it done in a longer holiday.

There's no magical phrase or response that'll stop the 'I want my ears pierced' requests – it's a lay-down-the-law issue really. It does help if you can give them an age when you think you will allow them to have it done (remembering that you'll have to stick by this).

# Bl**dy swearing

*'Within a week of my son starting school he came home with the delightful word "t*at" added to his vocabulary. Once I double-checked he really was saying that, rather than quack or twit, I was pretty horrified. I expected this sort of thing when he's older but not in reception!'*

Most of us, even those who swore voraciously in our pre-parenting days, make an attempt to tone our language down, if not with the arrival of offspring, then once they're showing signs of talking (who wants their baby's first word to be 'sh*t'?). Yet even the most restrained parent occasionally lets the odd naughty word slip and children inevitably copy. They're also bound to encounter swearing in the street and to an extent in the media, as well as in the playground.

What is socially acceptable has changed in recent years. I used to be threatened with a soap and water mouthwash if I uttered as much as a 'damn' or 'bloody' but in many families that's fine now. Ultimately, swearing is in the ear of the beholder and what you'll find OK might well be different to what I do, or other parents at school do or your mother-in-law does.

## Background info

Among our parent panel, 70 per cent allow no swearing at all, whilst 26 per cent only allow mild swear words such as 'damn'. The remaining 4 per cent don't object to any swear words.

## What the child psychologist says

Dr Jemma Rosen-Webb:

> 'There are a number of theories of how we acquire language but all of them include some role for what we hear around us. Children learn language by listening to others and copying. Young children often do not know what a swear word means but may have heard someone else (adult or child) use it. Older children may have been told it is a "bad word" and may use it as one of many ways of testing limits. Alternatively, they may start swearing so that they fit in with friends who are using these words.
>
> If you give a significant amount of attention to the swearing, e.g. you get upset and tell your child off, this might actually reinforce it. Instead, try to stay calm, tell them that that is a word you do not want them to use and why, and suggest an alternative word or phrase. For persistent and repetitive swearing, try to ignore it by telling them that you are only

going to talk with them if they can keep swear words out of it. If they continue to swear, focus your attention on something else or another child (if possible) who is behaving appropriately, and give your attention back to the child who was swearing the minute they stop.'

## What you can do about it

**Be a good role model** Don't say anything you wouldn't want your child to say. It's much harder to tell them not to use a word you use all the time. And they *will* repeat it and no doubt at the moment of maximum shame for you!

> 'Unfortunately we do sometimes swear (usually in the car) but we have explained to the children that it is wrong and we always apologise and say it was a mistake.'
>
> Allison (daughter 7, son 4)

> 'I've managed to modify what I say in front of him now – it is hard sometimes but I manage to use alternatives. My mother-in-law is always saying "Oh God" which I'm not that keen on for a 5-year-old – it sounds odd and he goes to a C of E school so I'd worry that, knowing my luck, he'll start saying it on a day the vicar is in doing assembly!'
>
> Vicki (son 5)

**Provide alternative words for when they need to let off steam** If they seem to need something to say when they drop their chocolate bar or whatever, steer them towards words like drat, blast, bother, sugar and the like – for some children a silly word like sausages will turn annoyance into giggles.

*'They can say "Oh my gosh", as we used this to stop them saying "Oh my God".'*

Allison (daughter 7, son 4)

*'We try and use inventive ways of suppressing swearing by using comical phrases. Any swear words used are questioned and strictly cautioned.'*

Sasha (sons 9 and 7, daughter 5)

**Be mindful for older primary schoolers** They aren't going to want to say something 'uncool' in front of their friends. By this age, they might be cynical about your suggestions but there is still hope until they reach secondary school. One strategy some parents go with is to make up a word that sounds like it could be a swear word (something short such as 'blig' or 'gub' sounds about right) and suggest that it's a bit naughty. Not everyone will like this idea, as it still encourages the intent of swearing even if the meaning is not there.

*'I made up a word, and gave the impression that it was just a little bit naughty (I did Google first to check it wasn't actually something offensive in another language!). Lo and behold they started saying it. I didn't think it was realistic to ask them not to swear at all and I'd rather they had an expletive to use when they are annoyed.'*

Chris (son 10, daughter 7)

**Explain why and stand firm** If you don't want to allow something another child they know is permitted to say, explain why and stand firm asking your child not to say it. They are going to hear swearing more and more as they get older (on TV and in films, and on the street/at school), the best you can do is educate them as to why swearing isn't nice.

If they use a word you don't like, perhaps explain to them, in an age-appropriate way, what it means and why it can be offensive to some people. Sometimes just giving the meaning of a word can take away the mystery and stop them saying it.

**If you do allow swearing, make your child aware that there's a time and a place** Explain that what might be OK in your family might not be for others and that sometimes they will need to tone down their language, e.g. no religious-based swear words if they visit a church with school.

*'I'm not that bothered by the occasional word, but I tell them that others do mind, so to use swear words wisely. I also don't want every other word to be swearing.'*
Jo (sons 15, 11 and 3, daughter 9)

*'Milder words I don't mind, as long as they understand not to use them in the presence of certain people (teachers, Granny, etc.). Context is important. Their granny and most people in their school are Christian, so I don't allow them to use words like God, damn, etc. unless they're at home.'*
Amanda (daughters 11 and 8)

**But remember younger ones might need a blanket rule**
If they can't discern when it would be appropriate or not, this might be safer.

*'Our approach is that if I wouldn't want them to say it in front of my mum, they shouldn't be saying it at all!'*

Jo (daughter 6, son 2)

**Speak to their teacher** If your children are repeatedly bringing home inappropriate language from school, speak to their teacher. Yes, they're meant to expand their vocab at school but not like this! Most primary-school teachers will have a sympathetic ear and try to work out where this is coming from, or might have a chat with the class about bad language.

**Don't overreact** If you sense they're simply doing it to wind you up, say your bit about why it's wrong and declare that you will ignore them (then stick by it) when they use that word. They might get bored if they're no longer getting a reaction from you.

**Consider having a family swear box and donating the proceeds to charity** Older children who get pocket money, and the grown-ups, might be expected to put a small amount in the box for bad language.

---

**Early dating**

A few children start talking of boyfriends and girlfriends in the primary-school years. We're not going to go into too much detail here as on the whole this usually means they just like the look of someone. At most they might ask to go on a date and anything more than holding hands or a peck on the cheek would be very unusual.

Your best bet initially is to check what they mean by 'boyfriend'/'girlfriend' or a 'date' and gently ask what they do

---

when they're together. It is very unlikely that most 11-year-olds are up to much but if you are concerned that the relationship is already less innocent, it could be time for another chat about relationships and sex.

## Further reading

- *So Sexy So Soon*, by Diane Levine and Jean Kilbourne, published by Ballantine Books.
- *The Period Book*, by Karen and Jennifer Gravelle, published by Piatkus Books

# 7

# Gadgets and games

**Screen time, mobile phones and internet safety**

# The big issues

- ✔ Screen time
- ✔ Internet safety
- ✔ Mobile phones

I remember my brothers and me watching telly and arguing about whose turn it was to actually *get up* and change channel (with no remote controls, no wonder there was less childhood obesity) or whether to switch off *Swap Shop/Grange Hill* and play asteroids on our new Atari console instead.

At some stage, Mum would threaten that we'd 'get square eyes' if we didn't switch it off or if we sat too close to the screen. We really believed her. Tell that to kids today and before you've finished the sentence they'll have Googled 'square eyes', discovered it is not a known medical condition and, erm, that you made it up.

That Atari and our 1980s remote control-less but colour TV seemed the height of electronic sophistication when I was little but my mum's concerns were relatively simple compared to the tech-related worries modern parents face now. Should we allow our children a mobile phone of their own, and if so who pays? How can they use the internet safely without us constantly watching over their shoulder? And how do we ensure we all still talk to each other despite the onslaught of so many screen-based diversions?

# Screen time

*'Though I have strict viewing times, I do find the one thing he gets stroppy over is the TV, especially at the weekend. He would watch for hours if I let him.'*

Computers are undoubtedly a learning tool and even TV programmes and games can be educational at times, a way to bond if you watch/play together, and darn useful for staving off boredom when it's throwing down for the tenth consecutive day of the school holidays.

But equally, most of us are aware of the downsides of screen time – such sedentary, passive pastimes (arguably excluding the likes of Wii Fit) can contribute to obesity and, according to research, leave children lacking the skills to entertain themselves, concentrate or relate to others without the assistance of some gadget or other.

So, how do we get that balance right? How much *is* too much? And in the words of one of my childhood favourite programmes, *Why Don't You*, how can we encourage them to switch off the TV set and do something less boring instead?

## Background info

- In a 2009 survey of British children by Childwise, those aged between 5 and 10 watched an average of 2.5 hours of TV per day (interestingly the boys sneaked slightly more in than the girls at 2.8 versus 2.2), 69 per cent of 5–10-year-olds had a TV in their bedroom and 77 per cent had a games console at home (but of course it might be for the whole family/ an older sibling). 63 per cent had one in their own room.

- Among our parent panel, 67 per cent place a limit on TV watching/screen time for their children. The most common limit across all primary-school age groups is 'one to two hours per day'. Other parents take more of an ad hoc approach:

*'I don't set specific time limits – I think it makes it more forbidden and therefore more attractive, so I try to be quite informal and, again, we agree things as each request comes up. I rarely refuse a computer request for homework, but I may refuse if they are just larking about on it.'*

Josie (son 13, daughters 10 and 7)

*'We don't have set restrictions. We have an agreement that they self-regulate, and if they spend an unreasonable time on it, then we will have to introduce some limits, which will be more restrictive than they are currently allowed! This seems to work.'*

Jackie (sons 9 and 6)

- Nearly everyone who does have a limit allows exceptions when their child is ill and, for some, during school holidays.

*'During holidays, at grandma's house and if my daughter is ill, then TV is unlimited.'*

Sara (daughter 10)

*'Occasionally we have film-night Friday, where she can stay up a bit late for movie and snacks.'*

Kelly (daughter 6)

## What the child psychologist says

Dr Harriet Tenenbaum:

'For this age group, no more than two hours a day split between television viewing and computer use for entertainment purposes (i.e. excluding using the computer for schoolwork) is reasonable, and possibly less on school days. Of course when children are ill, a parent can make exceptions. Allowing children to split the time as they wish between TV and the computer gives them some autonomy to choose between the two and can work well.

The type of television viewed is as important as the total time. For example, research suggests that educational programmes are related to school success, whereas entertainment (e.g. sports, cartoons, music videos) and general-audience (i.e. not children's) programmes may have the opposite effect. This could be because children might not understand general programmes as well, and adults might not interact with children whilst watching them.

Research also shows that violent content (sometimes even present in children's cartoons) can increase violent behaviour. Watching something together makes it easier to monitor for this. Meanwhile, where some programmes show beneficial positive behaviour (e.g. altruism or helping people), watching together allows you to reinforce these messages.

Adverts can be a particular concern, especially for younger children. Below the age of 8, they might not understand the intent and context of advertising and even above 8 can be susceptible to messages that you might not be comfortable with.

Computer games and the internet are similar to television in having both potentially positive and negative effects. Studies suggest some games can increase spatial skills and those played as a team with other computer users foster cooperation. Instant messaging of friends can improve literacy and help maintain close friendships. On the other hand, as with TV, violent games increase children's aggression, so it's important to monitor games to check for violence – perhaps play each one yourself before deciding whether it is appropriate.'

## What you can do about it

**Establish ground rules** These might be 'No TV/games/ computer use until homework is done', 'No TV when we have visitors' and setting limits, either based on time allowed or number of programmes/games. It makes sense to lump TV and gaming time together. Your kids will know what they're allowed and, as long as you stick with the rules, it should cut down conflict and pestering for more screen time in the long term.

> *'He knows he's only allowed three (short) TV programmes a day and then it has to go off. Occasionally he'll try it on and attempt to talk me into another but it's very rare and mostly he knows the rule's a rule and there's no point asking.'*
>
> Vicki (son 5)

**Set a good example** If you've always got the telly on/are constantly surfing the web, it's harder to credibly limit your children and also gives the idea that TV should be a constant presence or that life's about being glued to your computer all day.

> 'They have made a few comments about why I'm on the computer surfing the web so much but they're not allowed to for as long. I have had to cut down and save some of my surfing for the evening when they're in bed!'
>
> Anna (sons 10 and 6, daughter 8)

**Keep the TV and computer close to where you normally are** (See below for more about TVs and computers in bedrooms.) It's easier to monitor how much and what they're looking at if you're nearby/can at least pop your head around the door occasionally.

> 'The kids have their own computer in the playroom but I check in on them and what they're looking at pretty frequently.'
>
> Jacqui (daughter 11, son 9)

**Accept that a little TV/gaming/'interneting' is important for their social life**

> 'Even when we were children, I remember feeling left out for a few months when my parents banned TV – it would be even worse now. The important thing is that they have enough screen time/gadgets to "fit in", but not so much as to be detrimental to school work/family life/health.'
>
> Anon (sons 10 and 7)

**Make use of TV on-demand/record programmes** When the programme finishes it's easier to switch the TV off rather than facing requests to watch the next thing.

*'We only watch TV over the internet now … the TV doesn't stay on after the programme is over. It takes an effort to find something else to watch and it's never on in the background.'*

Sara (daughter 10)

**Plan with them what they'll watch** If TV is causing trouble, it's worth sitting down with a TV guide, and talking through which programmes they might watch that week. This way you're agreeing set limits, making them feel involved in decisions and, crucially, making it easier to turn it off afterwards, plus ensuring they actually watch something they really enjoy.

**Watch/play with them, at least sometimes** OK, so this isn't always achievable and you might not relish hours of CBBC on end but, at least occasionally, watch whatever they are watching. This means you can ensure it's appropriate viewing and might allow you to use any issues in the programme positively. So, if there are stereotypes you don't like or bad behaviour, discuss them together. Talk about the adverts and what they're for/the messages they are sending out.

*'I normally leave him to it if he's watching a kids' channel. But I was wondering where he was getting some of the attitude he was showing and when I did sit and saw one or two of the programmes it was clear. They aren't inappropriate for his age but some of the characters in the programmes are a bit of a pain and knowing this we had a talk about it and their and his behaviour.'*

Catherine (son 8)

**Encourage non-screen-based activity where possible**
It's healthy for children to be able to entertain themselves away from a screen but sometimes they need a bit of a nudge in the right direction. Keeping them busy with other activities is likely to mean they simply have less time for TV, although watch out for that over-scheduling issue at the other end of the scale (see page 56, on extra-curricular activities).

**Have an occasional no TV/games/computer day** You'll probably get a few groans for this and it might be a bit of an effort for you but it could get them into the habit of trying other activities out.

---

**So, how much is too much?**

There are no official guidelines for children's TV watching in the UK but the American Academy for Paediatrics recommends a limit of two hours a day for this age group.

It makes sense to apply this to all screen time, not just TV – anything fairly inactive which involves sitting with a gadget: computer use (other than maybe for homework research), gaming and DVDs. You might still find two hours too much for younger ones on school days – 14 hours a week is a significant chunk of their time awake and at home.

---

**TVs and computers in bedrooms**

If too much TV is bad, having a set in their bedrooms is, it seems, worse still. Studies suggest children with a set in their bedroom spend 1.5 hours extra a day watching TV, and bedroom TVs are associated with higher rates of obesity and poorer school performance. It also makes monitoring what/

how long they're watching for difficult. The situation with computers is much the same.

Asking for a TV of their own is prime pestering subject matter, though. Your children might well claim 'Everybody at school has one'. So do they? Research by Ofcom in 2009 showed 47 per cent of 5–7-year-olds and 67 per cent of 8–11-year-olds had a TV in their room but that's still quite a lot who don't and certainly not 'everybody'. It's also worth noting that of those who do have their own set, only 7 per cent of the younger ones and 20 per cent of the 8–11-year-olds actually have a digital TV service on it. Anecdotal evidence suggests some of these children's TVs might only be hooked up to a DVD player, limiting what they can watch to pre-selected programmes/films.

If you're feeling pressured, explain that different families have different rules and why you aren't comfortable with them having a TV/computer in their room, e.g. it makes it hard for you to check they aren't watching anything inappropriate or which might upset them. Add that they are welcome to watch TV/use the computer downstairs, where it's more sociable anyway.

A strop may ensue no matter what you say with this one. If you do want to compromise, perhaps allow a TV linked to a DVD player only and not tuned in with an aerial, as above, or let them have an MP3 player for music and story CDs instead.

# Internet safety

The internet is both a blessing and a curse for parents, but what's certain is it's central to modern family life. Whilst it's enormously welcome for researching homework projects or answers to those endless, challenging questions our children pose, for many of us this sits alongside concerns about inappropriate content and predators in chat rooms.

## Background info

- In 2009, Ofcom's research showed 16 per cent of 8–11-year-olds had internet access in their bedrooms, as did 3 per cent of 5–7-year-olds.

- Most parents trust their child to use the internet safely: 80 per cent with 8–11-year-olds and 63 per cent with 5–7-year-olds in the survey do. Only 45 per cent have parental control settings (see below).

- 24 per cent of 8–11-year-olds had a social networking profile in 2009.

- 43 per cent of the parent panel's children had an email address by the end of primary school.

## What the child psychologist says

Dr Harriet Tenenbaum:

'Children's social understanding of the internet lags behind that of its technical complexity. For example, a 10-year-old might have a fairly sophisticated understanding of the internet itself but it isn't until at least two years later that they have sufficient social understanding about dangers such as privacy issues and not until much later that they understand dangers stemming from identity theft and child pornography. Parents need to discuss these issues with children to help them understand the social dangers of the internet.

However, it's also worth considering there is *not* a plethora of internet-initiated assault against young minors from adults posing as children or adolescents to seduce children. In these circumstances, children usually realise they are communicating with adults. Studies in the USA show the vast majority of sex-related internet crimes are actually perpetrated against adolescents.

So, other than monitoring for inappropriate content now, your job with primary-school children is to set the foundations for safe use of the internet over the coming years. Talking about sex with unknown people in a chatroom, email, via instant messaging, or social networking sites increases risk.

A more pressing problem for younger children is cyberbullying – online bullying. And unfortunately for those bullied online, it seems that they are frequently bullied at school too, possibly by the same people.' [See page 20 for more on bullying generally.]

## What you can do about it

**Set up parental controls on the computer** This is a bit of a no-brainer and I'm sure most of you have done it but if you haven't it doesn't take long and should be relatively easy. Note, though, that these controls are not always 100 per cent watertight, so you do still need to keep an eye on things, remaining nearby when the computer is in use.

> 'We keep the computers downstairs, so that we can just pop by and see what they are up to. If they are on my husband's computer upstairs they have to keep the door open.'
>
> Josie (son 13, daughters 10 and 7)

**Educate where necessary** With older children, start to educate them about the dangers of the internet, so that you lay the foundations for safe usage once they don't want you looking over their shoulder all the time.

> 'We constantly speak to our children about e-safety
> – they are not allowed into chatrooms. We keep
> communication about computers going – they all know
> it's easy to stray into inappropriate fields and we have
> said if that happens to tell us.'
>
> Josie (son 13, daughters 10 and 7)

**Consider the pros and cons of their own email account carefully** Do they really need one at this age? Bear in mind that they could receive inappropriate spam, even if filters are set up. With younger children if you really want them to have an email account, ask them to confirm things with you before opening email file attachments – these could be a virus or inappropriate content even if they appear to be from known addresses.

> 'I thought it'd be fun for him to have his own email
> address so we set it up – he emailed his cousin in
> America and that sort of thing. The problem was the
> spam-type messages coming into the account – some of
> them were not the sort of thing I'd want him seeing. We
> have carried on using it but I have to sit with him when
> he is emailing now, which is not ideal.'
>
> Catherine (son 8)

**Discuss the risks of social networking with older children**
Talk in a measured, age-appropriate way about the dangers

of this – perhaps that sometimes people tell lies on the internet and that children should never arrange to meet up with someone they've met online as a very small number of people might want to harm them.

**Educate them on ways to keep information safe** Doling out personal data online adds to the risks.

Advise them never to give out personal information online without checking with you first, even if it's to someone they think they know:

- Specify what you mean by personal information (name, age, address (email and home), phone numbers, school, telling people where they are going, giving out photos or videos of themselves or others).
- Tell them not to fill in questionnaires or surveys without checking with you first.
- Make it clear they can tell you about anything they've seen online that has scared or worried them.

**Think about passwords** Consider asking older children using password-protected sites to keep all passwords the same so you can see what they're doing.

> 'As well as having "Internet Nanny" software, I insist that all passwords are the same, so I can look at what is going on. I pay for broadband, I bought the laptop, so I can look at what is on the laptop at any time.'
>
> Caroline (son 10)

**Watch out for other devices with internet access** These could include games consoles and mobile phones. Set up parental controls on these too, especially because, being so portable, they're more likely to be used when you're not around to supervise.

# Mobile phones

Mobile phones pose yet another technological dilemma for parents. According to one major phone network operator, 9–11-year-olds are the fastest-growing group of new users.

Mobile phones are undeniably handy in case of an emergency when your child isn't with you, but given worries about their safety, especially for younger ones (research suggests associations between children's mobile phone use and brain tumours) and the whole issue of managing who pays for calls, it's a tough decision as to whether and when to get them one.

## Background info

- According to Ofcom, in 2009 11 per cent of 5–7-year-olds had their own mobile phone and 54 per cent of 8–11-year-olds.

- Parent panellers' children who have a phone of their own typically got them at age 9 or 10. Most of those whose children didn't already have a phone said they would get them one when they started secondary school.

- Many of the parent panel give their older children a small allowance for calls – particularly for practical or emergency calls. Often this is in the form of a Pay as You Go card – say £5 a month – or a very basic line-rental package. After that's used up they have to pay with pocket money.

## What the child psychologist says

Dr Harriet Tenenbaum:

> 'Children might want a mobile phone for prestige, sociability and reassurance reasons. In a study of mobile phone use in year 6 children, 47 per cent said that they actually used their phones to call their parents most frequently out of anyone, and 38 per cent reported that they had used their phones for a perceived emergency (some of these calls were for emergencies and others were in situations like parents forgetting to pick them up).
>
> A few of the children in the study had received frightening messages (possibly bullying) and some had had their phones stolen. It would be wise to teach children about the dangers of being unaware whilst on the phone, such as when crossing roads, and about setting a PIN number to prevent use by others.'

## What you can do about it

**Think about and discuss why they want one** Is there really a genuine need/benefit to them having a phone of their own – especially if they're not travelling to school/ out anywhere without a grown-up just yet? Is it the 'But everyone's got one' factor – in which case they probably don't anyway (see statistics above). Who would they call?

**Have a compromise** If you don't want them to have their own phone yet, a compromise might be a spare mobile for the family which they can borrow when needed, e.g. when they start venturing out on their own.

*'I don't think they really need a phone until they get into using it socially – maybe in a couple of years. At the moment we have a spare one which the older two share and they take with them if they go somewhere which might mean they need to phone us.'*

Susie (daughter 13, sons 10 and 8)

**If you do go ahead, set ground rules up front** These could be about what the phone can be used for and who they can call. Is it for emergency use only or can they use it socially, e.g. to text friends? When can they use it – do you really want them texting their way through Sunday lunch?

*'It's only if she really needs to call me urgently, if she is worried about something while she is out with another family. She is also allowed to use it to SMS her dad when he is away!'*

Angila (daughter 8)

**Agree who will pay for line rental top-ups/calls at the outset** Once you've agreed the budget, make it clear that any extra costs will have to come from pocket money/ savings/their piggy bank. Pay as You Go phones make it easier to cap spending, but as these phones don't come with itemised bills you won't have the same opportunity to monitor who your child calls (if you want to do this) as you would with a monthly contract. Some operators allow parents to set a monthly spending limit on contract phones.

> *'I buy him £5 of credit a month and if he wants any*
> *more he has to pay for it himself from pocket money.'*
> Caroline (son 10)

**Limit use where possible** No one knows for sure that mobile phones are safe for children this age – for peace of mind, ensure they aren't talking on it for hours. Ideally it should be for short calls/ emergencies only.

**Watch out for internet access on the phone** It could allow them to see inappropriate content when you're not around/are unaware of it. Set access controls.

**Consider a special children's mobile phone** These are beginning to appear on the market. Not everyone approves, but if your child is going to get a mobile phone anyway they might be a better alternative to grown-up ones, thanks to some useful features (they can allow you to restrict who your child can call more easily, have no texting function and no web access).

**Teach your child to be sensible when using the phone so as to not attract unwanted attention** Sadly children do get mugged for phones after school, so ensure they know not to flaunt their phone, even if it's not the flashiest model on the market. Also remind them to pay attention when crossing roads if they're on the phone, or ideally not to use it when crossing roads.

# 8
# Tricky questions

**Sex and drugs
(not rock and roll)**

## The big issues

✔ Sex

✔ Drugs

✔ World events

As soon as children can talk, they seem to be able to identify the single most excruciating question to ask you at any given time. It might be in front of the mother-in-law or in an eerily silent waiting room. There are the questions that make you blush ('Mum, what's a w**ker?'), the ones that leave you wondering how on earth they've heard of such things ('Dad, what's crack cocaine?') and those that you might want to know the answer to yourself ('*Does* God exist?').

Once you've composed yourself from the shock of being asked some of these things, you've then to balance saying so much that their young heads can't cope, against satisfying their quest for knowledge and preventing misunderstandings. The tricky question really then is how to do that.

## Sex

*'My eldest at 9 asked "What is a blow job?" and "Do you do it with Dad?" Very embarrassing!'*

The questions about sex (albeit indirect ones) often begin with the simple 'Where do babies come from?' Some parents stick to talk of 'special cuddles', 'seeds and eggs', others prefer introducing a little more detail from the start.

Sooner or later, though, most children want to know

more and questions can get quite complex. We might live in a relatively liberal era, but discussing sex with our kids remains awkward for many, with varying degrees of blushing, sniggering or resorting to endless euphemisms.

## Background info

- A survey by Marie Stopes International suggested only a third of parents of 7-year-olds had talked to them about sex; the figure was still only 42 per cent for 12-year-olds.

- Among our parent panel, of those who had already discussed puberty and sex with their child, 28 per cent first talked about this when they were 6 or under, 30 per cent when they were 7 or 8, 32 per cent when they were 9 or 10 and the remainder when they were 11.

## What the child psychologist says

Dr Harriet Tenenbaum:

'The tone in which parents discuss this topic is so important. A study of university students showed that those whose parents discussed sex in a friendly manner when they were younger engaged in less sexual activity in secondary school and at university and were more likely to use contraceptives than those whose parents used a more contentious tone. So discussing sex early on does not mean your child will start having sex younger.

The key is to ensure the lines of communication are open. One concern if you don't discuss sex with children is that they will turn to peers for information and that information might not be factually correct.'

## What you can do about it

**Don't dodge their questions** No matter how tempting it is to change the subject, if your children are old enough to ask, they deserve an answer, albeit pitched at a level that they'll be able to understand and which is appropriate.

> *'If they are old enough to ask, then you must give them the answers honestly. I feel it's important if the boys are coming home with misinformation from the playground that I put them right, so they aren't learning the wrong things.'*

> Lynsey (sons 10 and 7)

**Decide whether you want to raise the subject yourself** Some children just aren't as curious as others about all this. If yours hasn't picked your brains for at least the basics by the time they're heading for the end of primary school, consider introducing the subject yourself. They might already know more than you think, though, and will probably have had some sex education lessons at school. Even if they have had sex education classes at school (and most will have), it's still worth starting a dialogue and setting the foundations for when they're older.

> *'We brought the subject up and A was happy with that, as he had heard things in the playground and wanted to know more.'*

> Sharon (sons 10 and 9)

**Think about using books to support your discussion** Books on sex education for children can be a godsend if you find it all a bit embarrassing. But don't rely on them alone; it's really important to make it clear that you are still available to answer any ensuing questions, now or when they're older.

*'Give them time to think about the information you have given them and allow them time to ask questions.'*
Susan (sons 11 and 7, daughter 9)

**Keep things age appropriate** It makes sense to introduce a bit more detail as puberty looms but they might only need the basics before then. Every child is different, so gauge their reaction and maturity level when deciding where to pitch the conversation.

**Try not to show any embarrassment** If you find talking about sex awkward, showing this could make your children think there's something to be embarrassed about, rather than all this being a natural human function. So be careful about the message you are conveying.

*'I have to try extra hard to be matter of fact when he asks me about how babies are made, etc. My natural reaction would be to get all flustered and embarrassed but I don't want him to grow up with the same hang-ups and attitude to such things as I had!'*
Vicki (son 5)

**Think about whether you (and your children) prefer informal or formal terms for body parts** Children and indeed parents invent all sorts of bizarre names for boobs, bums and other bits. There's nothing wrong with using whatever names suit you and your kids but it's good for them to be aware of the proper, commonly used terms too, in case they're mentioned by other children.

> *'If I'm talking seriously, I use the correct terms as I don't want them to be embarrassed about them. If we are joking around then we tend to use silly names.'*
>
> Coralie (sons 7 and 5)

> *'I think that once we start talking about sex, we will change to the "proper" names. It is only right that they know about them so that they understand them when they are used among their peers/at school.'*
>
> Angila (daughter 6)

**Don't worry about discussing sexually transmitted diseases** It's not necessary at this stage. It might be best left until closer to the time that your kids are likely to actually be having sex (OK, they start young these days, but hopefully most 11- and-under kids aren't actually 'doing it').

**Focus on the relationship** If they ask questions about same-sex relationships or you want to discuss this, it might be easier to focus on the relationship itself rather than the sex at this age.

> *'We explained that some men loved men and some women loved women and this was different from the love they felt for each other as brothers or their uncle and it was also different from the friendships they had with other boys. We also explained they had sex in a different way but we did not go into any detail.'*
>
> Sharon (sons 10 and 9)

*'[I said] simply that sometimes adults like adults of the same sex as opposed to someone of the opposite sex. This is fine and nothing to be worried or silly about.'*

Susan (sons 11 and 7, daughter 9)

---

**Preparing for puberty**

The age at which our parent panel first discussed puberty properly varied but the vast majority had had a chat about it with their child by the time they were 9 or 10. This sort of thing is normally covered as part of the school curriculum – if you're unsure about when and how this will be done, ask the teacher. Again books can be helpful but it's important to be there to answer questions and chat too.

---

*'[We talked about puberty] at around 9 with the eldest two. I told them that as they got older their bodies would start to change to get ready to become an adult. I explained what changes would take place and that everyone would go through it but at different times.'*

Susan (sons 11 and 7, daughter 9)

*'I had very early periods myself so I was pretty determined to tell her before she was 9 (I was 9 when mine started). She was 8 when we had the proper chat.'*

Anon (daughter 13, son 9)

*'From time to time, puberty-related matters crop up, e.g. [I might say] "They're called sanitary towels and I use them for my period" but I gave a proper explanation to my oldest girl when she reached 9.'*

Mandy (daughters 9 and 6)

# Drugs

*'I didn't think drugs had come up on her radar screen until one day she mentioned something that was actually quite ill-informed. I didn't know whether to cover it in more detail or brush over it.'*

Drugs of the non-medicinal variety hopefully aren't something most under-11s have personal experience of in their everyday lives. However, with media coverage and drug education programmes going on in schools, the majority of older primary-age children usually have at least some awareness of their existence. Which means you could face some questions – the key here, as with sex, is to lay the foundations for a healthy attitude for when they're older.

## Background info

- According to a survey of 9–11-year-olds by Life Education (see below), when asked 'What drugs do you know the name of?' 56 per cent of children could name four or more unprompted. Cocaine was the best known, with 71 per cent of children mentioning this.

- Other research, meanwhile, suggests that younger primary-school children have little awareness of the subject.

- These differences fit with the National Curriculum, which mentions the topic of illegal drugs during Key Stage 2.

- Very few of the parent panel introduced the subject with under-12s but they do respond to any questions about drugs openly on an ad hoc basis.

## What the drugs education expert says

Stephen Burgess of the charity Life Education, which runs drugs-related education sessions for primary-school children:

> 'It's no use pretending that children don't know about drugs. They do, and in order for them to approach the potentially challenging period of adolescence knowing the full facts rather than responding to hearsay and peer pressure, we need to reach children early – at primary school.'

## What the child psychologist says

Dr Harriet Tenenbaum:

> 'Research suggests children's views about drugs at an early age are more influenced by what parents say than what their peers tell them. It isn't until 13 that children are more influenced by peers. The key point here is that early conversations are important for helping children form their opinions.'

## What you can do about it

**Stick with the basics for now and keep it age appropriate** You're setting the foundations for later on rather than needing to provide the finer details of each narcotic substance's characteristics.

*'I've explained that there are drugs that are medicines to make you feel better, and other types of drugs that people take because they make them feel good. I've explained how a person can become addicted to drugs and can't stop taking them even though it makes them ill. I've also said that they should say no if ever offered drugs.'*

Mandy (daughters 9 and 6)

## World events

*'Quite often if there's been a natural disaster somewhere, he'll start worrying about it. I never know how much to tell him as I think he's old enough to be aware about this sort of thing but unfortunately he's not always able to keep the risks of it happening to him in perspective.'*

News stories about disasters and wars can be scary enough for grown-ups, never mind children. It's tempting to turn the TV off when the news comes on if they're around (and with younger ones this might be wise) but even if you do, some stories seep into their consciousness regardless.

I remember my parents used to let us watch the news in the 1980s without any explanation or reassurance, and I spent much of the decade terrified of nuclear war and had regular nightmares about it. Nowadays most of us are a little more aware of how the news can alarm children but it remains a fine and hard-to-navigate line between educating them about the world and frightening the life out of the poor darlings.

## Background info

- Among the parent panel, 23 per cent never let their children watch the news, 59 per cent let them watch it but turn it off if something particularly disturbing comes on, whilst the remaining 18 per cent let them watch it without any screening.

- Among their children, 20 per cent have had nightmares or expressed significant fears after watching something on the news, with natural disasters being the most likely thing to have made them anxious, followed by child abductions.

## What the child psychologist says

Dr Harriet Tenenbaum:

'Children are exposed to current events, such as war, regardless of whether parents bring the subject up or not. It is important to talk to them about these topics because not discussing it simply allows them to develop even greater misconceptions. For example, young children do not have a good understand of geography and may think that a war is geographically close to them, when it's not. One suggestion is to take their lead by asking what they know and if they have any questions.

Adults can reassure children, but be careful not to make promises that you cannot keep. If they seem very concerned, you can help them draw pictures or role play to express their feelings.

Another thing to remember is that parents cannot control the images shown on television, so you may wish to keep the television off for a while if a major disaster occurs. On the other hand, you can preview images in a newspaper and show them to children to help you explain, and print images tend to be less frightening for children.'

## What you can do about it

**Consider limiting exposure to the 'grown-up' news** Do they really need to know the details of all the bad stuff that goes on just yet? Especially when they might be too young to put the risks of it happening to them in perspective.

*'We have been known to switch the TV off at news time if there's something disturbing going on. We will talk about bigger stories but I think some of the pictures on TV aren't appropriate for younger children.'*

Laura (daughters 10 and 8, son 6)

**Be prepared for hearsay** Be aware that even if you haven't mentioned a big news story, they might hear about it anyway. Ask them if anything is worrying them if you know there's a big news story that they might have picked up on.

*'I didn't even think to mention it when there was a major earthquake as he's so young and I don't want to freak him out but he came home from school talking about it as they'd discussed it in assembly and had an event to raise funds.'*

Vicki (son 5)

**Look at child-oriented news** This can help explain things in a more appropriate way when they want or need more information.

> '*Programmes like* Newsround *and* First News [www.firstnews.co.uk] *are excellent at presenting the news in a way they understand and my sons both watch and read them.*'
>
> Sharon (sons 10 and 9)

**Provide reassurance and help keep worries in perspective**
Keep your responses age-appropriate – try to anticipate what might scare them and keep things in perspective, e.g. explaining that whilst these things do happen, they are very rare and you will do all you can to keep them safe.

> '*I do tell them the reason it's on the news is because it is a one-off/unusual event and it is very unlikely to happen to them or people they know.*'
>
> Jo (daughter 10, son 8)

---

**Other tricky questions**

No book can provide a foolproof prescriptive way to answer every question your kids will throw at you – your responses will depend on your personal beliefs and your child's understanding – but here are some ideas on a few common questions.

Remember you can always say you'll think about it and get back to them later, but make sure you do – if they're anything like my rather persistent son, they will ask again at some stage anyway.

*What happens when people die?*

Clearly your answer to this will depend on any religious views

---

you do or don't have. If you don't have any, there's nothing wrong with saying you don't know.

Note: dealing with bereavement is covered further in Chapter 10.

> *'I can't answer this one with anything other than "I don't know" as we're not religious and I really don't know.'*
>
> Nicky (son 9)

### Are you going to die?

It's unwise to lie about this, even if your 6-year-old might dissolve into floods of tears on learning that you are not immortal. Instead, the best you can do is provide reassurance that it's relatively rare for people to die before they are old and you plan to be around for many years to come.

> *'He asked when I might die and I said usually people are really quite old when they die and by then he'll be all grown-up and have his own family. He still seemed a bit worried, to be honest, but hasn't mentioned it again since.'*
>
> Sarah (son 7, daughter 4)

### Is there a god and why do some people believe different things?

Again, this is obviously down to your own religious views, but it's wise to make them aware that not everyone thinks the same.

> *'[I've said] different people believe different things about God and how you should live your life. Some people believe that there are lots of different gods and some believe that there isn't any god. I tell them when they grow up they'll be able to think about it and decide what they believe.'*
>
> Mandy (daughters 9 and 6)

> *'I've told them that everyone is different and believes in different things from small issues like a favourite band or food to a different way of life or religion, and that this is OK.'*
>
> Sharon (sons 10 and 9)

*Why do people get divorced? Why don't X's parents live together?*

'Children are raised in different environments and ours (a mum and dad who live in the same house) is not necessarily the norm. And as long as a child is loved and cared for and is happy, then it shouldn't matter who brings them up. We've had to talk about this as one of his best friends is being raised by his grandparents.'

Frankie (son 4)

'Some parents don't live together – sometimes they don't want to be married any more. A's daddy still loves her and she still sees him, it's just that they don't live in the same house any more.'

Mandy (daughters 9 and 6)

# Further reading

• www.lifeeducation.org.uk

# 9
# Financial matters

## The price of being a parent: pocket money, presents and parties

## The big issues

- ✔ Pocket money
- ✔ Christmas and birthday presents
- ✔ Birthday party politics

Imagine a bank where there are far more withdrawals than deposits, where the customers demand money that isn't even theirs and are frequently rude to the staff – who in turn, rarely get a thank you, let alone a salary. Welcome to that infamous Bank of Mum and Dad – there's a branch in every family home, waiting to dole out cash for pocket money, presents, parties and even handouts via the tooth fairy.

## Pocket money

*'Apparently all his friends get pocket money now, so I feel under pressure to give him some. I guess I'll have to give in soon but have no idea how much is appropriate and whether it's a good idea to link it to chores or behaviour.'*

Pocket money gives young children early lessons in saving, budgeting, value for money and mental arithmetic challenges such as 'How many 50p's do I need to buy a rocket to take me to the moon?'

Whilst many teenagers garner amounts bordering on small countries' GDPs, and which can make noticeable dents in family finances (£80 a month is not unheard of, and we're not just talking about Russian oligarchs' children here), newer customers to the Bank of Mum and Dad are usually satisfied with fairly modest sums. And the other good news is that comparing the amount of pocket money they receive is *not* a hot topic in most primary playgrounds.

## Background info

- The Halifax Pocket Money Survey has collected data on weekly sums received by children for over 20 years. Whilst the average 1987 8–15-year-old got £1.18 to spend on sherbet dips and a copy of *Bunty/Beano*, by 2010 the equivalent figure was £5.89 – an increase considerably higher than inflation over the period.

- The Halifax research doesn't cover younger children but our own survey did, and found that most of those who get pocket money receive much smaller amounts – reception to year 2-ers are typically on £1 to £2 a week, and plenty get just 50p, and are no doubt pleased as punch with it, bless them.

- Among our parent panel, 45 per cent don't give pocket money, either because they haven't got round to starting yet or prefer to buy items for their child on an ad hoc basis.

Of those who do:

- 53 per cent pay pocket money depending on behaviour being good enough; for example:

*'For all three girls, pocket money starts at £3 per week and reduces depending on their behaviour during the week, whether they did as they were told the first time they were asked, keeping their rooms tidy, etc.'*

Sarah (daughters 9, 8 and 5)

- 29 per cent make pocket money dependent on chores being done. Tasks that commonly fed into pocket money or earned extra included:
  - setting the table
  - tidying bedrooms
  - emptying the dishwasher
  - feeding family pets
  - sorting out laundry.

Purely for amusement, we asked 'What's the most ridiculous thing your child has spent their pocket money on?':

> 'She swaps £1 coins for 5p coins with her very knowing older sister.'
>
> Issy (daughters 7 and 5)

> 'More pink bloody hair accessories. How many does one little girl need?'
>
> Debbie (daughter 7)

Generally, popular pocket money items are comics, chocolate, and among the girls, endless bits and pieces from a certain girly accessories shop presumably founded by someone called Claire.

## What the child psychologist says

Dr Jemma Rosen-Webb:

> 'Families obviously vary in their views on if and when to give pocket money, how much and whether it is tied to chores or behaviour. If it is linked to behaviour, research has shown

that this will be much more effective if your child is rewarded and working towards something rather than having things taken away. For example, they could have 20p for every day that they do a particular chore.

Bear in mind that this sort of thing needs to be done consistently and could be a lot of work for you: if you're good at keeping track of things by using stickers, charts, etc., then great; but if you're likely to forget, it may be better to keep pocket money separate from any other strategies you are using to change behaviour. If children compare with their peers, use it as an opportunity to either review whether your decisions have been fair or discuss with them that different families do things in different ways.' [For more information about rewarding good behaviour see Chapter 1.]

## What you can do about it

**Work out your pocket money strategy** Do you want it to reward good behaviour or be automatic? The time-honoured tactic of reducing pocket money in response to misbehaviour is popular but, as our expert says above, positive rewards are usually preferable. The mere threat of docking pocket money will galvanise some children into sorting themselves out, though, so it is, of course, your choice if you think this works for you.

**Or perhaps link it to jobs around the house** Some parents believe children should just do their bit as part of mucking into family life. Others are happy to incentivise their child to do chores with extra pocket money. Although using money for specific tasks is a good introduction to how the world of work operates, the danger is that children start refusing to do anything for free.

One approach is to clearly define everyday unpaid chores. These might include making beds, putting toys away at the end of the day and clearing up after dinner. Other 'extraordinary' jobs – washing the car or helping with a big clear out – can then be paid for.

> 'He gets money for jobs. Loading the dishwasher is 20p, sorting washing and putting it in the machine is 50p, washing up is 20p, dusting the TV snug is 50p.'
>
> Jo (son 6)

> 'They do earn money (say 50p or so) if they help with a selection of household chores. Other chores such as keeping bedrooms tidy, setting the table, etc. are done automatically.'
>
> Petra (daughter 8, son 5)

**Use pocket money as a way to educate children** This might include things like shopping, consumerism and 'good value'. Offering a little advice when they're at the shops spending pocket money helps with their personal finance education ('Darling, are you really sure you want to buy that plastic dinosaur/lurid hair clip when you have 27 already?')

> 'We try to teach them the value of money with their pocket money and encourage them to consider what will last longer, e.g. sweets versus a colouring book.'
>
> Lisa (daughters 6 and 5)

*'Sometimes we interfere if they want rubbish and try to explain that cheap stuff can be poor quality and will break easily.'*

Coralie (sons 7 and 5)

**Decide whether you want to suggest a proportion is saved** Perhaps provide three money boxes or envelopes – one for saving, one for spending and one for giving (to charity, for presents, or both).

*'If they're saving up pocket money to buy a larger item, I help them keep track of how much they've got compared to how much they need, using a little chart. When they reach their target, I take them to the shop and get them to hand over the cash so that they feel fully involved and maybe a little proud of their achievement.'*

Victoria (daughter 11, son 7)

**Opt out of regular pocket money or go with a different approach** This can give you more control over what money is spent on but on the downside doesn't help kids learn so well about saving and budgeting.

*'We use a little notebook as a cashbook. They get credits and debits rather than cash handed over. It gives me some control but still allows them to learn about saving and spending.'*

Deborah (son 9, daughter 6)

*'They don't get regular pocket money yet. This is mainly due to the fact we are a somewhat forgetful family: we forget to give, they forget to ask!'*

Petra (daughter 8, son 5)

# Christmas and birthday presents

*'Some of the kids at school seem to get so much. I can't afford to match it and even if I could, I'm not sure I'd want to spend that much anyway.'*

Of course, the joy of Christmas and birthdays isn't solely about presents, presents and more presents, but when you're a child, they don't half help. Opening everything on Christmas morning to see if Santa has managed to deliver that much-coveted new toy is surely the stuff memories are made of.

But should you choose or get them to write a list? What if they long for something you can't afford or don't want to buy? How much do other families spend and do kids compare anyway?

## Background info

- Among our parent panel, Christmas spending per child was typically between £50 to £100 for a main present plus stocking fillers, although as you'd expect there was lots of variation and a few 'outliers' (one splasher-out spent a hefty £350 per child, compared with another parent who paid £25).

- According to our parent panel, their children's present envy tends to focus on the items themselves rather than the cost – think coolness factor rather than financial worth. A relatively cheap item can have as much playground kudos as something pricey. Very few of our parent panel had experienced children complaining about not spending enough on presents.

*'Do they compare presents with other kids? No, not that I've heard. Occasionally they'll comment on some great present, but they've never implied that they should get the same.'*

Marcia sons (11, 9 and 6)

*'They tend to be more interested in the number and desirability than the financial value of presents.'*

Issy (daughters 7 and 5)

*'She has one friend in particular who always seems to get very fancy, expensive presents but it's not a big problem. She mentions it and has a little sulk maybe but is still always happy with her own presents.'*

Suzy (daughter 7, son 4)

## What the child psychologist says

Dr Jemma Rosen-Webb:

'Think about your motivations for giving expensive gifts. Perhaps you don't live with your children and want to let them know they are loved? Maybe you are making up for things you felt you missed out on during your own childhood? Remember that children value things that do not always cost a lot, and spending time with you is top of that list.

It's better to keep presents for occasions (e.g. Christmas, birthdays) and incentives for "good" behaviour or consequences for "bad" behaviour separate. All too often, parents use Santa not visiting as a threat for a good few months of the year. This is a consequence that is not immediate enough to be effective. It is also one that most people are extremely unlikely to follow through on. If you did, it would be harsh and unfair.'

## What you can do about it

**Consider asking for a present wish list** You could ask for this in order of preference – especially good if the little darlings' requests are getting out of hand and they seem to want the entire stock of the toy shop.

> *'She has a wish list. I choose a few things from it. Surprisingly they're not always expensive.'*
>
> Hina (daughter 8, son 4)

**Help them understand *why* they can't have everything they want** Whether this is due to financial circumstances or just out of principle, it's a far more useful life lesson than a blunt no, and an opportunity to focus on less materialistic aspects of Christmas and birthdays, such as being together with family and friends and eating special food.

> *'If they start complaining that some other kids at school received more, I explain that perhaps someone less fortunate than them didn't even have what they got.'*
>
> Jo (daughter 10, son 7)

**Seek compromises** If they're desperate for a present that costs more than your budget, suggest combining Christmas and birthday money, asking grandparents to contribute to the cost of the larger present instead of a separate gift, or going second-hand.

**Deal with indecision by introducing 'Santa's closing date for present applications'** If your youngster changes their mind every day/hour/minute about what they want for

Christmas, introduce a 'closing date' sometime beforehand, after which they can't change their mind.

**If necessary, try to agree on a budget with any ex-partner/ the grandparents** This cuts down the scope for comparisons and guilt, although in practice it can be a sensitive issue. If your ex showers the kids with expensive gifts you can't afford or don't want to buy, explain to your children why you've spent less and don't feel guilty. If someone needs to resort to trying to buy affection, attempt to rise above it!

**Use Christmas or forthcoming birthdays as a trigger for purging old toys** Do this especially if your lot are reluctant to give away stuff they've outgrown. Any proceeds from selling larger items could be added to their present budget.

*'I introduced a rule this year that just before Christmas and his birthday we find any toys which he's grown out of or aren't being used. We send these to the charity shop – it means he's not hoarding loads and loads of stuff.'*

Vicki (son 5)

---

**What the parent panel said about Christmas present budgets**

*'We probably spend about £50 but it varies wildly. If what they really want is a £14 Furby, then we get that and don't worry about the fact that it was substantially less than £50. However, on other birthdays we've bought items we thought they wanted and ought to have, like a bike or a camera, that have exceeded the £50 limit.'*

Issy (daughters 7 and 5)

---

> *'I try and spend about the same on both of them. Every year, I pledge not to go mad and every year when it comes to the wrapping up, I realise just how many bits and pieces I've stashed away.'*
>
> Jane (sons 11 and 6)

## Is the chubby man in red and white really just Grandpa dressed up?

The average age for discovering Santa Claus is not real (sorry to disappoint any of you who were still believers until the start of that sentence) was 7 among the parent panel's children. Sadly my own cynical son stopped believing at just 4. One tactic if they ask if you believe or if Santa exists and you don't want to lie is to reflect the question back to them and ask what they think.

> *'If it means they get a present, they'll believe in anything!'*
>
> Amanda (daughter 10, son 8)

> *'I told my eldest that once everyone in the family knows, there'll be no point my giving them stockings any more. In other words, if he grasses me up to his brothers, he won't get a stocking. That has so far successfully stopped him from blabbing.'*
>
> Marcia (sons 11, 9 and 6)

## The depth of the tooth fairy's pocket

When I were a lass (I grew up in Lancashire, so reckon I'm justified in talking like this) the tooth fairy gave us 10p a time. After her first deposit under my pillow, I decided to 're-invest' my 10p in some especially chewy toffees from the Woolworths' Pick and Mix to 'encourage' a few more teeth out so I could get my literally sticky mitts on the cash early. It didn't work but I remain proud of my entrepreneurial efforts to this day.

As with pocket money, increases in tooth fairy payments have outstripped inflation. According to 2008 research by the Children's Mutual, she hands over an average of £1.22 per tooth, making a total of £24.40 for a full set. We can't imagine most parents carefully placing such a precise amount under the pillow, so figure this means most go with £1 and a minority £2 or more. London children got the most, with 1 in 10 getting £5 a tooth.

The tooth fairy seems to inspire a fair bit of cheekiness among our parent panel families, and not just from the children:

> *'My 7-year-old found a stone that looked like a tooth and tried that. The tooth fairy wasn't fooled! She occasionally has a really busy night and has to collect teeth the next night, though ...'*
>
> Georgia (daughter 9, son 7)

> *'I found my teeth in my parents' side table drawer and recycled them a few times before they realised.'*
>
> Amanda (daughter 10, son 8)

The majority offered the round sum of £1 under the pillow each time, although a few gave up to £5 for the first tooth and one gave a more modest 50p.

> *'She got £5 for the first one because Daddy was playing tooth fairy that night (I was away) and he didn't realise he was paying way over the going rate. After the next tooth came out, I quickly declared that it was now £1 and the tooth fairy had made a mistake, perhaps because "he" was new to the job!'*
>
> Amelia (daughter, 9)

Most don't pay up for a rotten tooth taken out at the dentist but one or two said their fairy still would cough up.

> *'He had eight teeth removed under general anaesthetic and the tooth fairy nearly went bankrupt.'*
>
> Alexia (son 8)

> *'Yes, I would still pay up. Having the tooth removed would be punishment enough, surely?'*
>
> Louisa (daughter 5)

# Birthday party politics

*'I definitely find the birthday parties more competitive than the presents – probably because they all see each other's parties but not necessarily the gifts.'*

Even the sanest parent can go slightly mad when it comes to the annual birthday-bash-organising frenzy, what with deciding what to do, how much to spend and dealing with the political hot potato of who to invite. And all that before you've even sorted out food, party bags, cake and entertainment. Thank goodness birthdays are only once a year.

## Background info

- Of 211 parents (from across the UK) in a survey by Les Enfants (www.lesenfants.co.uk), 45 per cent spent between £100 and £200 on their child's party, 36 per cent spent less than £100 and 19 per cent more than £200.

- Of the parent panel, whole-class parties were common in reception but 50 per cent have actually never invited the whole class – either having no party or only a smaller one. Of the remaining half, 26 per cent stopped having whole-class parties in year 1, and 26 per cent in year 2, with the rest stopping in year 3 or after and just inviting a small group.

## What the child psychologist says

Dr Jemma Rosen-Webb:

'Birthdays and birthday parties do not have to be big and expensive for children to enjoy them. The most important thing for children is to know that their parents love them, want to spend time with them and are able to "hold them in mind".

Spending time with family and friends and being made to feel special are what's most important. This does not have to be expensive. Try to think what would be a treat for your child and ask them for ideas (of course, feel free to veto any that are too costly!).'

## What you can do about it

**Don't be afraid to go against 'the done thing' if it makes you and your child happier** If you know your son or daughter gets overwhelmed by big parties or prefers a smaller group, don't feel you absolutely have to invite the whole class because others have. Classmates' parents might be grateful for you setting a precedent for smaller events.

> 'This year not everyone had a whole-class party and we have decided not to. We asked him what he preferred – a special outing or the party, and he went for the outing – fine by me as it's much easier and probably cheaper.'
>
> Vicki (son 5)

**Remember that the most expensive parties aren't always the most memorable** You don't need to spend a fortune to give your child a lovely birthday. A simple tea party with some games, a sleepover or an outing with a best friend can make a lovely but more economical way to celebrate.

**Be sensitive about who you invite** It can seem the end of the world to a child left off a party list. Try to either invite everyone or a small group, so one or two children aren't excluded, and be sensitive when handing out invitations. It might be better to post them to home addresses rather than sending them via school if there's any potential for upset.

---

### Party bags

Like it or not, most children do seem to expect a party bag at the end of the birthday bash, although you could try getting away with a wrapped-up bit of cake and a balloon each.

Unfortunately the kind of junk that typically comes in bags isn't that popular with parents – be it toxic sweets or plastic tat. If you can balance something kids will love with something that will keep mums and dads happy without breaking the bank that's surely the ideal. I tried books at one of my son's party (they worked out at £1 each from an online book shop) – parents loved this but one or two of the kids demanded to know where the actual bag was! Another idea is to zip to IKEA or the like and get one small £1 toy each and you're done.

---

# 10
# Difficult times

## Parenting through bereavement and divorce

## The big issues

✔ Bereavement

✔ Divorce/separation

Helping your child through bereavement or divorce can be among the greatest challenges you'll have to deal with as a parent. And of course if your child is going through one of these upsetting events and its aftermath, you probably are too, making it all the harder for you to support them.

These subjects are big enough for a book in themselves and here we can only cover the basics, but you'll also find some references for sources of specialist support which can make a significant difference for children going through a difficult time.

# Bereavement

*'At first when my mum died, I found the children's reactions quite odd if I'm honest. One minute they'd both be in tears and the next they were off playing games as if nothing had happened. I was very, very upset about losing her, which they seemed quite thrown by, maybe because they think Mummy is meant to be strong, not in tears all the time.'*

Whether it's a friend from school, a beloved grandparent, or, more distressing still, a parent or sibling, children show and deal with bereavement in ways that can be hard to predict.

They do tend to react quite differently from adults and it's very normal for a child to flit between being upset and seeming like they've forgotten what's happened. The children's bereavement charity, Winston's Wish (see page 206), likens adults' grief to a sea that can be hard to wade through, whereas for children it's more akin to puddles they leap in and out of. One moment they're distraught, the next off playing with their toys or wanting to watch TV.

Given you are probably bereaved as well, you might feel you aren't able to do a good job of helping and supporting your children – this is one of those times where it's especially important to remember that you can only do your best.

Much of the advice here also applies to those with a seriously ill relative or friend.

## Background info

Among young people aged 11–16, 78 per cent have been bereaved of a close relative or friend (L. Harrison and R. Harrington, 'Adolescents' bereavement experiences', *Journal of Adolescence*, **24**(2), 159–69).

## What the child psychologist says

Dr Jemma Rosen-Webb:

> 'Research suggests that children have different understandings about death at different developmental stages. Between the ages of 3 and 5, they become aware that people can die. By the age of 6 they will start to understand that death is permanent and everyone will die eventually. Not until around 8 will they truly comprehend that people who have died no longer feel, think or hear. However, there are huge variations in this and each child's

understanding will also be shaped by their personal experiences of death and by emotional and cultural factors in the family.

Children (and some adults) may also have "magical thinking" about a death. This means that they may link something they did or thought about with the death. For example, "The baby died because I was angry at it for crying". This may lead to them feeling responsible for something they had no control over. Children are unlikely to tell you this, so it is important to explain that when people die it is not anyone's fault.

Depending on your child's age, temperament and relationship to the person who died, you could see a whole range of emotional expression. Some children become more clingy, others show their distress through misbehaving and anger. Some show their need for comfort through physical symptoms, such as stomach aches and headaches. Some can put their feelings into words, others find that much more difficult.

What you should tell your child about the death will depend to some extent on your own religious and cultural beliefs about what happens when someone dies. It is important to be honest, but talk at a level that is age appropriate. Children do not need to know the intricate details of how someone died but should be provided with some explanation. They might want to know lots straight away, or might need time to go away, think about it and come back with questions.'

## What you can do about it

**Seek support** For yourself if you're feeling very upset for an extended period, or if you find it particularly difficult to talk about events, and/or for your child if everyone in the family is finding it difficult to talk or you're concerned about the way they are dealing with things. Speak to your GP or contact one of the specialist bereavement charities that offer counselling services (see page 206).

> *'My daughters' real mother died (I am their stepmother) and my husband and I had the horrible task of breaking the news to them. We used the charity Winston's Wish for help – they have some fantastic resources for use with bereaved children. I think both girls have come out of the period of darkness as happy and secure children, which is all we ever wanted.'*
>
> Heather (stepdaughters 8 and 4)

**Encourage talking and show them it's OK to cry/be upset/ sad** Let them know they can talk about things whenever they want and that it's fine to show how they feel. Don't think you can't let them see you upset – you don't have to be strong all the time in front of the children. It's healthy for them to see you're sad too and that what they're feeling is normal in the circumstances.

**Deal with questions openly** Bereavement (and learning someone is terminally ill) can trigger a lot of questions about death from children; again this is normal. It's important to show that death is part of life. Discuss birds, flowers and insects dying as well as people and pets. If you simply don't know the answer to something they ask, don't be afraid to say things like 'It's hard for me to understand too' or that you actually don't know.

*'We worked really hard to answer all questions honestly and not to cover anything up. It was very hard, but worth it.'*

Heather (stepdaughters 8 and 4)

**Keep a close eye on their reaction** Bereaved children behave in different ways. Even the same child can react very differently at varying times. They might be fine and asking for dinner at 6pm and then dissolving into tears by bedtime. Some might start wetting the bed, not eating, or waking at night when they haven't done so for years. This is all normal, if difficult for you. If problems persist, again, seek support via your GP – counselling might be beneficial.

*'In the past year they have lost two grandparents, whom they were close to. On hearing, our then 10-year-old had a very surprising reaction – she received the news with a half-smile and seemed almost excited. We were shocked and angry about this, but as time progressed it became clear that she was genuinely upset. We weren't expecting her reaction, and probably upset her further by showing our anger. Both girls were very easily upset and clingy for a while afterwards and the younger one had a series of nightmares.'*

Mandy (daughters 11 and 8)

*'One of their grandparents has been diagnosed with cancer and the prognosis is not good. The younger one keeps coming out with comments and questions at odd moments, so he is obviously thinking about it. He has, however, become close to Grandpa recently, through*

*discovering a common interest in trains, so that is why he seems more concerned than his sister.'*

Lucy (daughter 6, son 4)

**Make it clear it was not their fault** They might think they were somehow to blame for what happened. Active imaginations mean that there can be quite obscure ways they believe this has worked, e.g. if only they had done better at school/not shouted at you, etc., the person wouldn't have died. Reassure them that nothing they said or did was the cause.

**Avoid euphemisms for death – they can confuse children** Saying something like 'Grandma has gone to sleep now' could make a younger child afraid of going to sleep. Explaining that the person has 'gone away' might make them think they left voluntarily, leading to fears others will die if they're away from them.

> *'They became worried that they would die, especially after someone told them that Gran had just 'gone to sleep and slipped away'. My younger daughter was frightened to sleep in case this would happen to her. We tried explaining that Gran and Granddad had been very old and ill, and had come to the end of their lives.'*
>
> Mandy (daughters 11 and 8)

**Help them remember** Creating a memory box can work well for primary-school-age children. They will be able to look at it when sad or when they want to remember the person. It could include poems or pictures they create, mementoes of their time together and photos – anything goes. Workbooks such as *Muddles, Puddles and Sunshine* (see page 205) can also help them talk about the death and the person they've lost. If it's too painful for you to do this with them, a close family member or friend could help work through the book/memory box and your child could then share it with you.

> 'The girls both created posters of their memories of Mummy, which we put at the front of the crematorium during the service. They drew pictures, put up photos of her and so on. The posters were then left with the flowers for all to see after the service.'
>
> Heather (stepdaughters 8 and 4)

> 'She released a pink heart balloon with a short message attached which she had written, to 'go to heaven' for Grandma. It seemed to help her say her goodbyes.'
>
> Claire (daughter 6)

**Prepare them for a death that's expected** It's tempting sometimes not to tell children about a relative or friend who is terminally ill (where it isn't otherwise obvious) but it can be helpful in the long term to be prepared and have a chance to say goodbye, even if it seems harder in the short term.

**Keep to their routine where possible** The certainty of knowing dinner will still be at six and bedtime at the usual hour is comforting for most grieving children.

---

**Should children go to funerals?**

Most experts advise it's best to let a child choose whether they want to go to a funeral, after explaining broadly what will happen and why. On the one hand funerals can leave some children even more upset but for others they help them understand the person is gone and it can be beneficial to be with family and friends who are mourning.

There's no right answer – it'll depend largely on your child and the nature of the relationship with the person they've lost. If it's someone close and it feels appropriate, you might want to include your child in some aspects of planning the funeral (e.g. choosing music) or they might want to participate in the service – perhaps writing something that can be read out (by themselves or someone else).

It's best not to pressure them, but follow their lead. Let them know they can change their mind even at the last minute and that whatever they choose is OK.

If you will be very upset, it's worth having a trusted family member or friend sit with your child. They can explain what's going on if needed, reassure them or take them out if they feel they'd rather not carry on part-way through.

If your child/you decide they aren't going to the funeral, bereavement experts suggest having some sort of memorial/ceremony for your children to participate in, whether it's planting a tree or sending balloons into the sky with a poem/message attached on tags.

### Fear of death and losing a parent

Many children develop worries about a parent dying, particularly after losing someone else close. If they ask you if you'll die, it's best not to lie and say it will never happen, but reassure them that it is very unlikely until you're older. If they still seem anxious, perhaps tell them what would happen, and any arrangements you have in place with guardians (note: any godparents have no legal status and are not automatically guardians). You might say something like: 'I don't expect to die for a very long time but if anything did happen to me, Auntie X and Uncle Y have agreed they would look after you'.

*'I know they worry about me dying (I'm widowed). And I can't promise them it won't happen. I've pointed out it's rare – I asked them how many children they know who have lost even one parent? So the odds on losing both are negligible, and they don't know anyone it's happened to.'*

Marcia (sons 11, 9 and 6)

## Divorce/separation

*'My daughter sat on the stairs and screamed that she hated me. She saw our separation as my fault. We had tried to keep our problems away from her, so it came as a big shock, even though I had talked her through things.'*

Parenting during and after divorce is complicated and draining, at a time when you probably aren't feeling your best. Even if they've endured years of arguments, squabbles and tension between you and your partner, it can still be quite a shock to children when they hear their parents are separating.

No advice here can magically wave away all your problems or your child's concerns and distress, but by communicating well and acting wisely you can at least go some way to minimising their upset and the disruption to their lives. And whenever possible, keep in mind that research suggests the two key factors in determining how deep and long-lasting the impact of a divorce will be on children are the quality of contact they have with both parents and the amount of conflict between them.

## Background info

Around 45,000 5–10-year-olds experienced their parents divorcing in the UK in 2008 (the most recent figures), according to the Office for National Statistics.

## What the child psychologist says

Dr Jemma Rosen-Webb:

> 'Children often feel that they are somehow to blame for their parents' divorce. They may become worried about upcoming changes and practicalities, such as who they will live with and where. They may have fantasies about parents getting back together or develop ideas of things they can do to make this happen. Towards the end of primary school, if given clear explanations by their parents, children are better able to understand that their parents have separated for reasons such as different goals and beliefs. Clear explanations will help them with the myriad of feelings they will be experiencing, e.g. guilt, anger, sadness.
>
> As with all difficult subjects, children need to be told the truth about what is happening but in a way they can understand. It is extremely likely they will have been aware of disagreements, arguments and tensions in the parental relationship. Being told about an upcoming divorce may bring some relief but also many concerns. Try to use child-friendly language, e.g. "Mummy and I haven't been getting along so well recently. We both love you very much but we are going to try living in different houses."
>
> If you have decided to get divorced, be clear that it will be forever and that as much as they might want you back

together again, there is nothing that they can do to change this. It's also worth thinking about what your biggest concerns would be if you were in their shoes, and trying to answer some of those questions for them, e.g. letting them know who they will still see (grandparents, aunts, uncles, cousins, etc.).

Try to think what they may be wanting to express but cannot find the words for, e.g. hurting a doll may be a way of showing they are emotionally hurt. Use play and stories to talk about some of the many mixed feelings that are likely to be around for everyone in the family. Adjustment will probably take a while.'

## What you can do about it

**Break the news together if possible** If only one of you can have the discussion or you literally can't bear to be in the same room, make sure the other parent talks with your children about it too. There is no right thing to say; however, it's wise to be honest (as ever, in an age-appropriate way), but don't overdo the details of your relationship problems. 'We are arguing too much and although we've tried to sort this out, we cannot', or similar, will be better than an hour-long discussion about exactly what, when and why.

> 'Initially we all sat down together and I told them that I didn't love Daddy any more and would be living somewhere else but that we both still loved them. At their age (7 and 5 at the time), it seemed best just to give facts of how it was going to affect their lives, focusing on the positive things (one-on-one time with

*each parent, two sets of presents, new house which would be an adventure, etc.). The single most important thing is to reassure them that you both love them and that they can talk about anything that is making them feel unhappy.'*

Jo (son 9, daughter 7)

*'I hated telling them. It was hard being in the same room as my ex at that stage, let alone working out what we would say without it turning into another argument. I'm glad we told them together, though, because it meant there was less room for one of us saying something different from the other.'*

Joanna (sons 9 and 6)

**Consider that timing can be difficult** Ideally, it's best to wait until practical details are firmed up. It's not always possible but, if you can, tell them sooner rather than later so they have time to adjust, e.g. to one of you moving out, but only once initial plans are firmed up.

**Make it clear it's not their fault** As above with bereavement, children need to hear that you are not separating because of anything they have done, as this is not always obvious to them.

**Reassure, reassure, reassure** Children whose parents are separating will need to hear that both of you still love them and are going to see them (assuming the latter is the case). They might worry about changes to school, moving house, not seeing grandparents, friends or even pets. Sometimes you simply won't have the answers yet – be honest if this is the case, but do try to resolve things as promptly as you can.

> *'It was my daughter's big worry that she would not see her dad when he moved out. I had to be honest and say that she would not see him every day now, which was very hard, but that she would still see him a lot.'*
>
> Clare (son 10, daughter 6)

> *'We certainly reassured them that they would still see us both and that they could call and if possible see the other parent whenever they wanted to.'*
>
> Jo (son 9, daughter 7)

**Communicate details of contact and living arrangements as early as possible** Given 'When/How much am I going to see Dad/Mum?' is a key source of anxiety for children after divorce, be as clear as you can about where/with whom your child will be when (a picture or written timetable might help younger ones).

If they'll stay regularly with the non-resident parent, make sure they have a place to leave clothes and toys. If they're going to have to move house or school, involve them in decisions where appropriate, without leaving them too overloaded.

> *'It was very hard as we didn't know initially what the arrangements would be, so although I wanted to promise he'd see me on specific days, I couldn't say. I tried to focus on the immediate future – that I'd see him on Wednesday and Thursday after school this week and that sort of thing.'*
>
> Michael (son 7)

*'They drew timetables with me of which days they were with their father and which they were with me, as we did different days alternate weeks. Each morning I would remind them what was happening after school that day. If there were changes to the normal rota, I would give them plenty of notice so that they were clear.'*

Jo (son 9, daughter 7)

**Keep daily routines the same if possible** If you can keep other aspects of their lives stable, it will help them through the transition.

**Remember it's quality, not always quantity** The quality of the relationship with a non-resident parent is what counts for children, not so much the frequency of contact. Even if it is not possible for your child to see the other parent much, phone calls, cards and photographs all help them know they are loved and not forgotten.

*'I nagged their dad about calling them as much as possible as he was useless about it at the start.'*

Kate (daughters 7 and 5)

**Try to understand your child's feelings and behaviour even if they come out in unexpected ways** Children react differently according to their personality, relationships with you and the other parent, and the nature of the separation/aftermath. Reactions can include denial, frustration, anger, blame or even silence. There may be an initial response and then quite a different one later on when they've digested things.

*'At first I thought it was all fine but it was only later on that there were more problems. Maybe it took a bit of time to sink in because my ex-husband was away a lot on business before we separated, so for a week or two it seemed like he was on a trip.'*

Joanna (sons 9 and 6)

**Ensure your children don't become pawns in arguments between you** It's stressful and upsetting for a child to feel they have to take sides. If you need to let off steam and complain about your ex, steer yourself towards friends or relatives, and do it out of earshot of your child, or seek professional support if you are finding it difficult to hide anger and frustration from your children.

*'Don't bitch about your ex to the kids. As they get older, children are able to see people's weaknesses for themselves and will appreciate the fact that you didn't point them out. Find yourself someone else who's been divorced – preferably years ago – since they'll understand what you are going through and be supportive without being bitter, or encourage you to chop your ex's Savile Row suits into shreds!'*

Kate (daughters 7 and 5)

**Think about professional help (if necessary)** If your relationship ended because of violence or fierce arguing, your child might have been affected by what they saw and heard. Consider getting help for you and them if that is the case. As ever, speaking to your GP is a good starting point.

**Other parenting post-divorce tips**

- Don't use your children to spy on what your ex is up to.
- Avoid criticising your ex-partner in front of your children – hard if you're feeling bitter, angry or abandoned but important for the sake of their relationship with them.
- Don't use your child as a weapon to punish your ex, e.g. by limiting access/contact.

**Divorce – other family members**

An aunt's, uncle's or grandparents' divorce might not be as life-changing for a child as their parents' separating but can still be confusing and difficult. Use child-friendly language to explain the situation honestly and provide reassurance, e.g. 'Auntie Kate and Uncle John have been finding it hard to get along and are going to live in different houses but you can still see them both and your cousins'. They might get concerned that you are going to get divorced too, so be prepared to reassure them on that too. If you are already divorced, bear in mind the new situation might lead to further questions about your own.

# Further reading

- *Help Your Children Cope with Your Divorce: a Relate Guide*, by Paula Hall, published by Vermilion

- *Muddles, Puddles and Sunshine: an activity book to help when someone has died*, by Diana Crossley, published by Winston's Wish, Hawthorn Publishers

- *When Someone Very Special Dies*, by Marge Heegard, published by Woodland Press

- www.crusebereavementcare.org.uk (bereavement support charity)
- www.winstonswish.org.uk (UK charity for childhood bereavement: also covers serious illness)
- www.divorceaid.co.uk
- www.fnf.org.uk (Families Need Fathers: help with shared parenting issues for mums and dads)
- www.gingerbread.org.uk (support and information for single parents)

# 11

# Other little challenges

## Lies, damned lies, bad habits and fears

## The big issues

- ✔ Horrid habits
- ✔ Fears and phobias
- ✔ Lying

Lots of the issues covered in this book fit neatly into themed categories such as eating, sleeping or school, but some do not. So here are the extra bits and pieces we didn't want to leave out as they're important – be they your son's constant nose picking, your daughter's hair twirling or both of them constantly squabbling with each other.

# Horrid habits

*'My son fiddles with his bits. I tell him "Leave it alone or it'll fall off". To which he replies his sister's already lost hers, so he'll be fine.'*

Children and horrid habits seem to go hand in hand (indeed many of their little quirks do involve fidgety hands), what with wiping snotty noses on sleeves, scratching bottoms, fiddling with private parts, biting nails, excavating nostril contents (and then, if you're especially lucky, eating them), picking scabs, sucking shirt sleeves ... I could go on.

Where habits are merely socially undesirable rather than physically harmful, should you try to change them and is there anything more effective than barking 'Will you stop doing that' 100 times per day?

## Background info

- Nose picking was the most commonly seen bad habit reported by our parent panel about their children, followed by nail biting and fiddling with private parts.

- According to one study, 91 per cent of adults pick their noses, so most of us are just as bad.

## What the child psychologist says

Dr Jemma Rosen-Webb:

'It's very common for children to develop habits that their parents find unpleasant, worrying or embarrassing. Whether it's thumb sucking, nail biting or any other habit, the chances are it has developed for a reason. Some habits bring comfort, for example when children are feeling tired, bored, nervous or sad. Sometimes habits provide relief from an uncomfortable state, e.g. picking out a big bogey that is making it hard to breathe! Still others may just feel nice, such as touching private parts. Or there can be a combination of factors.

Children may find their own habits or learn them by observing others – children at nursery/school, siblings or adults. As much as we like to hide it, many adults still have some of these habits, if not in public, in private. Sometimes when you think your kids aren't watching, maybe they are.

Habits are notoriously difficult to break because they are often internally rewarding, i.e. they bring comfort, enjoyment or relief. Ask yourself if it is really necessary to eliminate them altogether.

You may not be able to get rid of the behaviour even if you try but you may be able to shape it. Children do respond to feedback from their peers, so some habits may be changed in this way, e.g. a thumb sucker may stop sucking their thumb at school but still suck it at home. If you are concerned that the habit is causing a serious problem for your child, e.g. nail infections, severe head banging, raw skin from rubbing, then you should seek professional help via your GP or health visitor.'

## What you can do about it

**Look for triggers** Does it happen at a particular time of day? When they're tired or bored? Some bad habits are symptoms of stress, anxiety, frustration or tiredness. If that seems the case, help them to find other ways to manage those feelings. If it's a new habit or has increased significantly, could there be something going on in their life that's led to this? Take time to talk to them about anything that's worrying them.

**Reinforce and reward** Focus on praising them for not doing the thing that is annoying you and going with an alternative, e.g. 'Thanks for getting a tissue and blowing your nose' for a nose picker. Reward charts can work for this, if you're happy to go down that route. Whilst for most reward chart categories a star/tick for each day is fine, for habits you might need to start with a shorter period e.g. no thumb sucking from 4pm till 6pm. Then broaden things out once they're coping with that first step. If you are going to use a reward chart, involve your child in agreeing the steps, so they don't feel like it has just been imposed on them.

*'We used his reward chart to help stop him sucking his finger – it took a couple of weeks, so wasn't easy, and we also gave him plenty of praise.'*

Vicki (son 5)

*'She gets to use nail polish as treat at weekends for unbitten nails – it seems to work.'*

Claire (daughter 6)

**Pick your battles** If they have several bad habits, focus on tackling those that matter most – no more than one or two at a time. Consider whether it's really important if they occasionally do something that's merely mildly irritating for you to witness, such as hair twirling.

**Be patient** These habits can be hard to eradicate, but remember: if nothing is working, they'll probably grow out of it eventually on their own.

## Habit-specific fixes

**Try a non-toxic yucky-tasting paint-on substance for nail biters and thumb suckers** Some kids will get used to the taste or covertly wash it off, though. An alternative is to encourage them to make a fist with their hand to 'hide' their thumb or fingers when they get the urge. Thumb suckers who actually want to stop but can't can also try sticking a plaster on their thumb for a few days.

**Ensure bogey pickers blow their nose frequently if they're a bit congested** Some children pick when their nose is irritated. If they do it because it's just become a habit, direct their fidgeting to something else – you could encourage them to stroke their nose instead at first. If they do it to wind you up, ignore them when their finger heads up a nostril. Or tell them they can pick in the privacy of the bathroom and wash their hands after.

**Teeth grinding (bruxism)** At night this is rarely a problem and is usually outgrown, but if it's causing you concern because there's apparent teeth damage, discuss it with a dentist as your child might need a mouth guard. Daytime grinding is more likely to be about stress and needs treating like other habits above.

**Crotch fiddling** Fiddling with private parts is usually done because it feels nice. Sometimes children realise that it's also an effective way to embarrass you. Explain that it's not polite in front of others and if they want to they should do it in their room when they're alone. Avoid statements that might scare them or create a hang-up when they're older, e.g. it's dirty or their willy might fall off!

## Fears and phobias

'My younger daughter is terrified of dogs, to the point where it stops her wanting to go to places where there are likely to be dogs roaming about, such as the park.

My childhood was littered with fears: the dark, dogs, Daleks, and it wasn't just things beginning with D – there were also fireworks, fish (live, not dead), nuclear war (fair enough) and, rather bizarrely, escalators. My own son has now taken over the phobia mantle – so far we've had vacuum cleaners, hairdryers, lawnmowers, blood (he's not going to be a cleaner, doctor, gardener or hairdresser at this rate), broken glass (sensible) and bizarrely ... chickens (well, cockerels, to be precise, thanks to an incident when one crept up behind him at a farm and cockadoodledoo'd very loudly). Yep, some childhood fears can indeed be pretty odd and not always terribly rational.

## Background info

- Of the parent panel's children, 63 per cent have a significant fear or phobia.

- Their most common fear is the dark, followed by spiders and dogs.

## What the child psychologist says

Dr Jemma Rosen-Webb:

> 'Childhood fears are incredibly common. We all have an inbuilt fear response system that alerts our bodies to danger and prepares us to fight, flee or freeze in dangerous situations. For some children this system may be more sensitive than others. Additionally, some children are very sensitive to certain stimuli and this may make them fearful of particular situations or new experiences, e.g. being startled easily by loud noises, or not liking the feel of certain textures.
>
> All children look to their parents for cues about how to respond in different situations and they are often acutely attuned to their

parents' emotional state. It is therefore possible for children to learn fear of certain things by noticing their parents' fear.

In many instances there will have been a trigger event, e.g. being barked at by a large dog. If this is the case, children begin to avoid that situation and parents, wanting to comfort them, may help them do this. Some children may be able to tell you with words that they are feeling worried. Others may show it through behaviour, including becoming disruptive. Finally, if there is a heightened level of stress, conflict and anxiety at home, this may result in generally increased anxiety for a child.'

## What you can do about it

**Never ridicule your child's fears** Children rarely make this sort of thing up and even if it all seems silly to you, the fright they're facing feels very real to them. Teasing won't shame them out of it, and is unlikely to do anything other than upset and frustrate them yet more that you don't take their fears seriously. It's also worth bearing in mind that fears are a normal part of childhood – within reason.

**Reassure them** If whatever they're scared of is not really dangerous, reassure them of this. If it is, at least help put the risk in perspective. So perhaps 'Yes, lightning can be dangerous but as long as you take care not to be in a wide space it is very, very unlikely you will get hurt'. It's certainly worth having a discussion with them, when they are calm enough, about precisely what it is they're worried about.

*'With stuff he's scared of, we've realised we need to try to get to the bottom of exactly what the problem is to*

*help solve it. For instance, with spiders we were saying things like "They can't hurt you as they are too small" but it turned out he was worried they were going to bite him, so when we explained spiders in this country can't bite that had more impact.'*

Clare (sons 10 and 6)

**Be careful about transferring your own phobias** If you jump a mile every time a wasp/spider/dog comes near you, your child might well follow your lead. Children are still relying on us to protect them from danger, so if you are communicating something is harmful, they will likely believe you. If you can't hide your fear, it might be worth trying to overcome it yourself (see below).

**Don't assume they'll be afraid** Your child might not be scared of things that you expect them to be, so be careful what you say. Sometimes it's easy to condition a child into thinking they should be scared of, say, the dark.

*'C does tend to be scared of quite a lot of things but we are always careful not to assume something is going to frighten her – it puts the idea in her head. Sometimes she surprises us when we think something will freak her out and it doesn't.'*

Sarah (daughters 9 and 8)

**Try some gradual desensitisation** This is a grand term for getting them very gently used to the thing they're scared of. You take it one step at a time until they're no longer afraid. This can be hard work but is worthwhile if you're dealing with a fear that's quite severe or isn't going away on its own.

*'R was scared of dogs to the point where we'd have a massive trauma on our hands if one came close. We got her a book about dogs and read it together. Then we roped in our friend who has a very docile dog. We let R just do what she was comfortable with, which the first time was staying away and looking, but she managed to stay calm. Eventually she got a little more confident and was able to stroke him if I held her hand too. She's not exactly a dog lover yet and still becomes a little nervous but it's more under control.'*

Rebecca (daughter 10, sons 6 and 3)

**Seek help** Speak to your GP and ask them to refer you for specialist support if the fear is beginning to interfere with your everyday life or causing undue distress.

## Lying

*'I really struggle with working out when he's telling the truth or not and I think he knows it. Sometimes it's about things he shouldn't have done and I think he's scared he's in trouble, but other times it's much more random – like he says something about someone at school, which I later find out is made up.'*

At some stage, the majority of children realise they don't actually have to tell you the truth. They learn, often by chance, that you won't necessarily know they bashed little Johnny on the head first rather than the other way round, or that it was actually they, not their sister/brother/friend who scoffed all the chocolate when you weren't looking.

Having a persistent fibber in the family can be problematic but occasionally it can be surprisingly amusing – endearing even. Take the chocolate example – when they stand firm, insisting they 'Really, really didn't eat it all, honest, I promise' – with a big chocolatey smear all around their mouth.

I'd be lying if I said I never lie and herein lies the source of confusion for children – we all do it sometimes, to save face, to spare others' feelings ('What lovely singing, sweetheart' 'No, of course your bum doesn't look big in that, darling'). Yet there we are trying to teach them not to lie.

## Background info

- Children aren't actually terribly good at lying – research shows they only deceive their parents 15 per cent of the time. Sadly this doesn't seem to stop them trying.

- A University of California study suggested that 80 per cent of parents lie to their children (given how common 'social' white lies are, perhaps some of the other 20 per cent weren't truthful with the researchers?). Most of the very same parents said they teach their children it's wrong to lie.

- A survey by TheBabyWebsite.com showed that the most common fib parents come out with is that Father Christmas only brings presents to good children.

## What the child psychologist says

Dr Jemma Rosen-Webb:

'Nearly all children lie at some point or other. It may be part of normal boundary testing or an attempt to avoid being caught or getting into trouble about something. Socially acceptable behaviour requires a certain amount of lying or at least censoring ourselves from telling the whole truth. Without realising it, parents may encourage lying by asking children to tell white lies, e.g. "Now, whatever Aunt Dorothy has got you for your birthday, I want you to say you like it". It's important to explain the difference between white lies (e.g. to avoid hurting someone's feelings) and other lies.

Try to understand why your child is lying. Are they expressing an unfulfilled wish? Are they doing it to cover up an area in which they feel inadequate or to fit in with others? Acknowledge and try to help them with the reason behind it if there is one, while still having consequences for lying.

When you suspect they have done something wrong, remain calm and remember that children ultimately want to please their parents (even if it doesn't always feel like it). Put the emphasis on how happy you will be if they tell the truth. You may need to have a consequence for the thing they did (and possibly another one if they lie initially) but you can still reinforce being pleased when they tell you the truth. If chronic lying persists past the age of 6 or 7, it's worth seeking some professional help to try to better understand why your child is feeling the need to lie so frequently.'

## What you can do about it

**Watch out about lying yourself** We all tell white lies occasionally but if you frequently fib in front of your children or get them to lie for you ('I'm late for school because of the traffic' when really you all overslept), frankly you're setting a bad example. If you've had to lie for good reason and they've heard, perhaps explain to them why you did it.

*'I must confess I do tell the odd lie – things like saying we're busy when we're not, to get out of something I don't want to do – and he has started noticing. I'm trying to cut down or at least be more subtle, as I think my own parents set a bad example with me about this and I don't want to do the same.'*

Vicki (son 5)

**Discuss different types of lies** Lying to get out of trouble is very different from social lies to spare someone's feelings, and most primary schoolers should be able to understand the basics of this. Explain that socially 'positive'/white lies are different from 'negative' lies, which can mislead people or hurt their feelings. Give examples, such as saying they had a nice time to the host at the end of a party even if they didn't, or they like a present if they have it already. Then compare these to lies about fake illnesses, which make it hard for you to know when they're really ill and untruths about doing something 'wrong'.

*'He sometimes lies to try to get himself out of trouble. Often it is really pointless, like denying he did something I've actually seen him do just that minute. He almost does it as a reflex action.'*

Catherine (son 7)

*'I've had to talk to him about how some lies are good lies and some are bad. Even at his age he did seem to get what I was talking about.'*

Vicki (son 5)

**Call their bluff if you're pretty sure they're making something up** If you suspect they're, say, trying to pull a sickie to get out of school, a quick call to the doctor to make an appointment can sort out the truly ill from the fakers. You need to be willing to follow through with the appointment if need be though.

> *'Sometimes it's very obvious when she's lying but with some illnesses I find it hard to tell. A couple of times I've started getting out some medicine that doesn't taste that nice and all of a sudden she's magically better without the need for it. Luckily we haven't had an occasion when she has said she wants the medicine.'*
>
> Clare (daughters 8 and 6)

**Use stories about lying** If you've a persistent or problematic fibber on your hands, reading something like 'The Boy who Cried Wolf' (or one of the many other fables and more modern stories about lying) together might help. Be careful, though, as many such tales have alarmingly negative or unrealistic penalties for the liar; it's better to choose something more measured.

**Highlight your disappointment when they lie** A discussion about how much more disappointed you will be if they lie rather than tell you the truth about something they've done can encourage truthfulness. Highlighting that liars do usually get found out sooner or later can help too.

> *'I find talking quietly and telling them how disappointed I am by their deceit (a very nasty word) works much more effectively than having a screaming*

*match and losing my rag. Statesmanlike disappointment rather than screaming banshee – it works and they hardly lie.'*

Josie (son 13, daughters 11 and 7)

**Praise them for telling the truth** Do this even if they still need telling off about something they did. Quite a lot of children's lies occur when they panic about something 'naughty' they've done. If they tell the truth, a comment that you appreciate they were honest will reinforce the importance of not lying, without detracting from telling them off if they have done wrong.

> *'I hate lying and always bang on about how he will always get in much more trouble about lying than just owning up to something naughty he's done.'*
>
> Catherine (son 7)

> *'I always say what my mum said to me, that it is better to own up to something rather than lie and then get found out afterwards.'*
>
> Marian (stepdaughter 7, son 5)

---

**Sibling squabbles**

'She hit me first', 'No, he hit me first', 'It's my turn', 'No, it's *my* turn!' Multiply that by ten, and you've got the kind of not very civilised conversation that takes place in families with two-plus children across the land.

Now maybe a very positive person, with quite a long-term view, might see such squabbles as a way for children to learn to deal with conflict, but in the real world of everyday parenting dealing with constant battles and having to play referee can be exhausting. So what to do?

---

Tips for cutting down conflict:

- Where possible, set clear rules at the start of games or generally for the use of toys/gadgets/TV.
- Allow them to keep some treasured possessions as just theirs, but under the proviso that everything else is shared nicely.
- Accept that if there's something really popular (and affordable), you might have to buy one each to avoid arguments.
- Don't step in too quickly – leave them to sort out their own more minor battles and save involvement for the stage when they're about to kill each other! Teach them to ask themselves what they could do to make things fairer/who could go first, etc.
- If they aren't able to solve things and conflict is persistent, when they're calm, sit them down with you to discuss what happened, get them to empathise ('How do you think X felt when you broke his toy?') and work out what they could do differently next time.
- Learn what triggers their arguments to help find ways to prevent them – is it in the car or at mealtimes, perhaps? Always over the computer or what to watch on TV?
- Keep things fair. Try to ensure they get broadly similar amounts of attention, presents and possessions to avoid jealousy – inequalities can sometimes cause conflict. Also avoid making negative comparisons or labelling them.
- Distract them if they're about to start on each other. Or if it gets really bad, and it's possible, separate them for a bit until they calm down. The latter needs to be done fairly – don't send one to their room and let the other carry on playing if both were at the heart of the problem.
- Be realistic. Mild name-calling, the odd argument and the like are normal and fairly inevitable with children living in close proximity. Don't expect them to be best friends all the time, or even friends at all. But do look at ways to try to bring them together – a special outing they can both/all get excited about, for example.

And finally, keep in mind that siblings often go through phases of getting on better and worse. Those who fought the most as children might well still have close relationships with each other as adults.

## Further reading

- *What to Do When Bad Habits Take Hold*, by Dawn Heubner, published by Magination Press (a self-help guide to overcoming habits for 9–12-year-olds)